1988

PURE LIVES
The Early Biographers

P·U·R·E
L·I·V·E·S

The Early Biographers

REED WHITTEMORE

The Johns Hopkins University Press
Baltimore and London

The Johns Hopkins University Press, 701 West 40th Street, Baltimore, Maryland 21211
The Johns Hopkins Press Ltd., London

The paper used in this publication meets the minimum requirements of
American National Standard for Information Science—Permanence of Paper for
Printed Library Materials, ANSI Z39.48-1984.

Library of Congress Cataloging-in-Publication Data
Whittemore, Reed, 1919–
Pure lives : the early biographers / Reed Whittemore.
p.   cm.
Bibliography: p.
Includes index.
ISBN 0-8018-3548-8 (v. 1 : alk. paper)
1. Biography (as a literary form).   2. Biographers—History.   I. Title.
CT21.W5   1988
920'.02—dc 19   87-16822
CIP

To
HELEN, CATE, NED, JACK, DAISY

Contents

Contents

Acknowledgments

I am grateful to the staffs of the Main Reading Room, the Rare Book Room, and the Poetry Room of the Library of Congress, as well as to the staff of the McKeldin Library at the University of Maryland. I am also indebted to Professor Annabel Patterson for reading and commenting, most usefully, on an early draft of my manuscript. My thanks also to various readers of at least two final versions of the manuscript at the Johns Hopkins University Press, and to David Lundeen for the use of his excellent Samuel Johnson volumes.

PURE LIVES
The Early Biographers

Introduction

My focus in these essays is on five collections of early biographies, each originally set forth in several volumes, and each written by a single author. They are:

Plutarch's *Lives of the Noble Grecians and Romans*
Aelfric's *Lives of the Saints*
Vasari's *Lives of the Artists*
Holinshed's *Chronicles* (of the rulers of England,
Scotland, and Ireland)
Samuel Johnson's *Lives of the Poets*

I probably could not have found five duller-sounding titles than these (though Hesiod's *Works and Days* and Caesar's *Gallic Wars* compete); yet the books themselves are not dull. In our world of biography the best word for them may be *exotics*.

To provide a historical base I have grouped around them other biographers and a few influential figures in fields related to biography—notably Machiavelli, Cellini, Shakespeare, and Sterne—and have marched forward from Plutarch to the end of the eighteenth century as if I were writing a survey. But the result is not a survey. The essays will not serve as an introduction to the glory that was Greece or the muddles that came later, but I hope they will serve my purpose, which is to characterize and comment on the genre of biography before it became, in the opinion of many modern scholars, truly a genre at all.

Needless to say I do not share the scholars' opinion, for I see modern biography as deeply rooted in exotics. But I agree that a transformation within the genre did occur with, and immediately after, James Boswell. I am now at work on another volume that tackles the nature of the transformation after Boswell.

To come at biography by writing dozens of related biographies and giving them a common ideological and cultural context is a very different act from taking on an individual in isolation. The early biographers discussed here had in mind nobles, saints, kings, painters, and poets first, individuals second, and their emphasis was that of their times. Boswell and his successors reversed the emphasis, and in fact one of the most dogmatic biographer-critics of the nineteenth century, Edmund Gosse, said flatly, that "broad views" were "entirely out of place in biography" (*Encyclopaedia Britannica*, 11th ed.). My subjects here did not think so, and although a few distinguished single lives came out of the early period, the genre did not take its main principles from them. My five works are both distinguished in themselves and representative of the climate of thinking in Europe about the writing of "lives" before the transformation occurred. In other words they were not exotics when they appeared.

The climate that produced Plutarch's *Lives*, the work here furthest from us in time, was most obviously different from ours with respect to the individual, the self. That unlikeness has generally been perceived by modern critics as evidence of how primitive the self-understanding of even the most sophisticated ancients was, and while I propose to dispute this evidence in part, I must first try not to underestimate it. It clearly shows us that the ancients had wildly uninformed ways of dealing, for instance, with dreams, as well as quaint notions of the uses of the first person. It also shows us the ancients' odd disposition simply to deny that the self is significantly private. As noted by Jacob Burckhardt, who is commonly quoted in this connection, before the Renaissance "man knew himself only as race, people, party, corporation, family, or in some other general form." One does not handily refute Burckhardt. In many ways the cultural climate in the West right up to the Renaissance was indeed less self-centered, as well as less self-knowledgeable, than our own.

Still, the point needs to be made that the early instances of self-modesty were not nearly as clean and simple as Burckhardt's remark suggests. People did say "I," did write about their private lives in journals, and did have other than collectivist thoughts, ambitions, and lusts before the Renaissance; and especially for a well-traveled, well-educated, upper-class figure like Plutarch, the cultural climate must have been rather like our own, a climate that was really more than one climate, a climate that was surrounded by competing, countering climates (perhaps a better analogy would be weather systems).

Ancient biography was handicapped, I believe, less by ignorance of the nature of self than by conventions within which the genre worked, conventions of social observance that kept its practitioners from exploring many of the ramifications of self-meaning that were open to them. I would go further and say that our own conventions in the genre are, or can be, handicaps; also, that they are not as immutable and right for the genre as is now quite commonly assumed. For instance, the modern scholar Vivian De Sola Pinto has made our cultural devotion to probes of the individual the *sine qua non* of biography, asserting that the form "necessarily" developed late, since it "presupposes a society with a detached curiosity about life, and a conception of every human being as an individual worthy of respect." Heretically I have to ask Professor Pinto, How much of the world even now accepts such a premise?

And I have to follow up that question with a corollary: Do we not, even now, in many corners of the genre, think of individuals as being perfectly approachable as social figures first, and as individuals second? The answer is, Of course we do. I grant that when we do, the results can be dismal; much popular biography treats our culture's heroes as representative, unindividualized standard-bearers for the culture, and makes them look like perfect dolls.* There are worthier studies, though, in which a standard-bearer such as a president or a general is presented (as we keep saying) with his warts, even though he is a public figure doing his public thing.

The ancient biographers found fewer warts, and did not go to Freud for help in finding them. But they were not nearly as lacking in

---

* A good example is *Marie*, a popular 1986 movie derived from a popular semidocumentary book. The battered heroine of this story rises from nowhere to become a power in the government of Tennessee, and then to do, at great personal sacrifice, what modern heroes are expected to do—that is, fight the political machine with our culture's most sacred antigovernmental values. Marie is plucky, intelligent, tireless. Surrounded by gratuitous violence, hypocrisy, and plain mischief, she cleanly triumphs. The whole tradition of biographical encomium is relentlessly evoked, but the insights into Marie as an individual are childish.

self-awareness as Burckhardt and the others have maintained. The Burckhardt stance is derived from nineteenth-century scientism, and is particularly unaccommodating to the self-searchings, historically, of all the world's religions. It finds the word *soul* simply irrelevant, not seriously related to biographical investigation. Some of the ancient views of the soul may have been odd indeed, but even the oddest were in some sense investigatory of the self; and the views of sophisticates like Plutarch or, among the Christians, Saint Paul and Athanasius (see chapter 2) simply cannot be dismissed. That they are dismissed says more about the dismissers than about biography.

What has to be acknowledged is that ancient biographers felt constrained about man's physical self in ways that modern biographers are not. My anthropological guess is that the constraint can be traced back to the most primitive human taboos, back to when group solidarity began to question individual deviance. Stamping around tribal fires, muttering incantations, slaughtering sheep (or deviants), the purifiers began to cleanse us of our private selves and make us theirs.

In most cultures they still do, and the part of our private selves that is most in need of purification is usually the beast. The purifiers have never been reconciled to the beast. Their cleansing ceremonies have been relentlessly penitential about him, disciplinary with him, and sacrificial of him. Down the ages they have worked the beast over with everything from sacred emetics to Communion, and they continue to do so despite Charles Darwin. In these essays I will not go beyond the eighteenth century, but within my frame I will try to show the pervasiveness of the beast-purification itch while at the same time pointing to a few impure deviants, notably Sterne and Boswell.

In Western culture, where I must focus (since in the East the individual still is not respected enough to encourage biography of the modern kind), primitive purification rites spread out from religious temples into secular literature at a very early time—for convenience, let us say with the Greeks. For the Greeks, secular purification meant cleansing eminent persons of their faults by officially citing only their chief accomplishments and virtues, as with an inscription on a tombstone: probably the first form of biography. Then came lengthier encomia, in the form of speeches and testimonials, a tradition that is still with us, and still unreceptive to impurity (no derogatory remarks being appropriate here). Finally came the drama, and especially tragedy, with its provision that the beasts in mankind be allowed to appear, but only in order that they be exorcized.

And it was in the drama that Aristotle clarified the process on paper for us. His *Poetics* has been a purification bible for centuries, and is relevant for biography as well as tragedy.

Aristotle posited a hero who was a model human—that is, a superior being by reason of his character and position in life—who was nonetheless possessed of an impurity (his "flaw," his manifestation of the beast) that needed to be purged. And he posited an action, the purification rite itself, in which the purging took place. By that action the hero was in effect sacrificed to his own impurity, and the *audience* was vicariously purified as a result. Aristotle described the rite as an imitation of real human actions, an indication of how deeply rooted in human nature was the impulse to imitate. But he might better have called the rite a species of imitative or sympathetic magic, with the effects of stage action being psychically transferred to the audience through pity and fear. "Through pity and fear," he said, the action effected "the proper purgation of these emotions."

Unlike tragedy, biography did not, even in its early forms, *have* to be purgative, but it did need to present model humans as its subjects. For as with tragedy, the subjects of biography had to be superior beings, persons an audience could look up to and be purified by.

Also as with tragedy, the authors of model biographical exhibitions had to *believe in* the purification rite—that is, they had to possess what Aristotle described as a "grave" disposition. Aristotle dealt with these sober-sides historically, and from the tone of his remarks he obviously sympathized with them ideologically too:

> Poetry now diverged in two directions, according to the individual character of the writers. The graver spirits imitated noble actions, and the actions of good men. The more trivial sort imitated the actions of meaner persons, at first composing satires, as the former did hymns to the gods and the praises of famous men.

Thus did he dismiss comedy, and its authors, from the purification profession.

Certain observations that Aristotle did *not* make in the above passage must be noted if we are to understand the damage his dismissal produced. He did not say *in what respect* the grave were grave, the trivial trivial; nor did he characterize the nature of "meaner persons". But what he inadvertently admitted was that the trivial and the mean somehow produced satires. And there is the key: satire, satyr. When poetry rode off in two directions, the grave persons began to produce purifying tragedies, while the trivial persons began to celebrate (I think the word is just) unpurified experience—that is, the experience of humans shamelessly full of the beastly, as satyrs were.

Putting the trivial writers aside in this way (which was not, of course, exclusively Aristotle's doing) affected biography as much as tragedy. Not until modern times were the trivial writers inclined to work within the genre, or able to give it a base among the mean as well as the high minded, for ancient biography unequivocally adopted Aristotle's spirit of tragedy. It was a spirit not only grave but snobbish.

All of us who have lived with that spirit in courses in literary criticism know the *manner* in which Aristotle disposed of the beast in man, but it needs a brief summary here. Aristotle insisted that his tragic models be presented and evaluated in terms of their good and evil deeds, with as little beastliness intruding (their frailty, their flaw) as credible human traffic would allow. For the Aristotelian grave spirit the model self was always, properly, working to purify itself *of* self, not only by disciplining the beast, but also by being public spirited—that is, by joining the purifiers. Not to discipline the self-life by means of public service was, in essence, evil. A model self went about being good by assuming a virtuous public role as a military, political, perhaps judicial, leader in society.

This is where Aristotle's upper-class perspective entered. In his conception of self such a leader—that is, a being "highly renowned and prosperous," and possessed of clout—was the only sort of person with a potential for being meaningfully pure. Only great beings like that could even *have* character, since character, he said flatly, "is that which achieves moral purpose." And by moral purpose he insistently did not mean private purpose like the saving of a solitary soul; he meant purpose that influenced, carried over into, the lives of others.

Plutarch followed this Aristotelian gospel steadily in his *Lives*. So, if we can believe him, did most of the noble Grecians and Romans he wrote about, certainly the good ones. Their lives were purified by public service, with the leadership process making them high minded, rational, and disciplined whether they were or not. For Plutarch was committed to reporting and judging his nobles' flaws only when they surfaced in public. Luckily he was not a prude, and the process did not keep him from impressive thoroughness with many of his subjects. Many later biographical moralists have been more restrictive than he, and the result has sometimes been suffocatingly tendentious.

I myself have seen some of the suffocating. In my early teaching days at Carleton College there was a department of biography, and the College boasted that it was the very first department of biography in the whole academic (Christian division) world. It had been started in 1920 by one Andrew Vernon, whose theme about biography was that "[it sent] the student forth with the richest human material within reach." Vernon sent Carleton students forth with his rich material for five years, and then moved to Dartmouth to start a department of biography there. I do not know if either of these departments exists today (though each was endowed by enthusiasts, so something must still be happening), but I remember what the Carleton department was like when I arrived in the late forties. It was a one-man purificatory venture in the hands of a ministerial gentleman named Charles Mierow.

Mierow had been, I believe, a missionary, and he was certainly convinced that teaching biography was a missionary's game. He was a gentle disciple of Vernon's, a dedicated classicist, but an even more dedicated pietist. He was so earnest that some of the young teachers at Carleton—not I, of course—ridiculed his saintly tones. His class offerings were "Representative Moralists," "Representative Men of Antiquity," "Representative Men [of several other ages]," and, best of all, "Great Adventurers." (Like Plutarch, he included no women.)* In a book called *The Hallowed Flame* he later reported that he had managed to cover fifty great men, in all, in these courses. The book itself had in it biographies of eight of the fifty, religious leaders all (Jeremiah, Buddha, Confucius, Socrates, Epictetus, Saint Augustine, Mohammed, and Saint Francis). Each was properly directed upward and away from the beast; and so, Mierow delcared, were all great leaders. The biographies were therefore relentlessly exclusionary, being the Great Thoughts of these leaders untainted by lesser thoughts or by any mention of actions by them unsuited to their virtue. In his life of Socrates, for instance, Mierow did not even mention that Socrates and Alcibiades had more than a teacher-student relationship; Alcibiades was just a loyal, high-minded disciple.

Mierow's work was a late manifestation of the old biography, with

---

* Plutarch did write, however, a long essay on the "bravery of women." It was a summary account of legendary instances of the courage of women in many countries. No individual received extended attention.

its debeastification drive, and for the purposes of this account his view of the genre may be said to have been challenged, though not conquered, centuries before him. A commonly cited turning point in England was the late seventeenth century, when science was busy giving lessons in how to be empirical and inductive, and biographers were listening.* The resultant "new biography" gravitated to the short and unopinionated, and the practitioner who came closest to the collectivist format chosen by my five biographers was probably John Aubrey.

Aubrey was no purist himself, and seems to have written many of his 462 "brief lives" under the influence of a hangover. He did not choose his subjects for their gravity and purity, and he did not pass moral judgments upon them, but simply loved, as Edmund Wilson said, to "compile gossip about famous men [and women], and note their peculiarities." Nor did he group his subjects according to their life roles. He preferred to write about miscellaneous persons he met, say, at parties. He was simply not methodical. Yet some of the detail he picked up said much in small compass, and usually it was thematically neutral or antipathetic to virtue. There was, for instance, Sir Jonas Moore, who cured Sciatica "by boyling his Buttock"; and Venetia Digby, who died suddenly by poisoning, and "when her head was opened up there was found but little brain." I will briefly return to Aubrey and his kind, as harbingers of the new, in chapter 7.

◆ ◆

By the time of Johnson and Boswell, purification of the Mierow kind had become fairly rare in biography. Johnson himself, though no prude, was as great a conservator of the restrictive moral tradition as anyone, but another old kind of purificatory principle remained at work in the genre. It was a kind less attractive to the world's uplifters than goodness—one might even call it a purer kind—but it was a kind that Boswell, ushering in exhaustiveness in biography, did a good deal to undermine. I mean the complementary kind of clearing away of underbrush, getting down to cases, disposing of the irrelevant, the

---

* Dryden is said by some to have been the first to use the word *biography*, though in using it he spoke of the old dispensation rather than the new. His remarks and a number of representative short biographies can be found in Pinto's *English Biography in the Seventeenth Century*, which also has a useful introduction to the "new biography."

unfunctional. Down the ages we have had many, many expressions for this artistic, cleanse-by-exclusion impulse, this rage for order, and it is still with us, even among strident opponents of moral exclusions. But in biography it has, since Boswell, run into a strong countercurrent favoring inclusiveness, hence simple disorder.

On the one hand, modern biographers are apt to agree with Edmund Gosse that "broad views" should not be admitted, and on the other, they are likely to labor for no omissions at all, like Boswell. Even Boswell *qualified* the no-omissions ideal, saying that he was "exceedingly unwilling that anything, however slight, which my illustrious friend thought it worth his while to express, with any degree of point, should perish" (the equivalent of "all the news that's fit to print"). And Gosse, on the restrictive side, managed by a clever device to sneak broad views into his own short and limited autobiography, *Father and Son*. In general, though, modern biographers have found themselves caught between two principles, neither of which, by itself, they like much.

The Gosse device was that of the monograph. He confined his biography to an account of his difficult relationship, as a young liberal, with his fundamentalist father. A fine monograph it was, doing what we expect of monographs by providing an aura of meaning beyond itself while retaining a clean narrative shape. If Gosse had given us his whole life, the broad view he was sneaking in would have been lost in fluff, but sensibly he did not give us all of it. What we have is a simple chronological account seemingly of just one "soul . . . moving between two definite events, birth and death," but actually providing readers with a fine summary of the crisis in faith that science brought to nineteenth-century Western culture. Most modern biographers do not dare to be either so restrictive *or* so broad.

Another well-formed early modern volume, Lytton Strachey's *Eminent Victorians*, effectively imposed upon chronology a theme that is now dominant among psychobiographers (though sometimes not recognized by them *as* theme), and so gave the work a *rationale* for exclusion. With great craft Strachey presented the four lives in his volume—those of Cardinal Manning, Florence Nightingale, General Gordon, and Dr. Arnold of Rugby—as double lives. The doubleness he developed was the now excessively familiar ego-id, Jekyll-Hyde kind, but he made it unpretentiously the controlling pattern of each of the lives. Thus in the first paragraph of his life of Nightingale he pointed to the "popular conception" of Nightingale as a "saintly, self-sacrificing woman" who consecrated "with the radiance of her goodness the dying soldier's couch," but then went on to declare that "the truth was different," and that in fact Nightingale was possessed by a demon, one he later plumbed to impressive depths. Similarly he presented Cardinal Manning as outwardly a saint but inwardly Napoleonic, Dr. Arnold as a moral achiever who achieved the *wrong* educational morality at Rugby, and poor General Gordon as a pleasant chap who was dragged into a pit (Khartoum) he had not anticipated. The shaping force of these "lives" has seldom been matched. They are models of well-made biography because they rigorously exclude what Boswell was "extremely unwilling" to.

Unfortunately, biography now usually walks among us disguised as history, or political science, or psychoanalysis, or just exhaustive scholarship, with little visible shape except chronology. No other literary form has been so plagued by the obligation to include. Dutiful scholar-biographers now collect hundreds and hundreds of note cards about their subjects as they conduct their research, and dutifully put every single one into their texts. Monster biographies keep appearing that their authors do not even think of as reading matter. They are reference books, and if *everything* about their unlucky subjects is not in the pages *somewhere*—and discoverable via the index— then woe.

Early biographers did not try to be inclusive. Sometimes they omitted materials we think deeply functional to biographical understanding, and sometimes they included materials (like oracular prophecy) we think nonsense; but these writers were at least aware of biography as a genre, a *form* of human statement, in a way that too many modern biographers are not. The dream of the clean and clear in art and literature remains a good one, but at the moment only the biographers with limited objectives, like Gosse or the "vita"-mad contributors to biographical dictionaries, are dreaming it.

I

Plutarch and the Dream of Virtue

Modern biographers speak condescendingly of Plutarch (A.D. 46–120). He was too anxious to assess his subjects ethically, they feel, to have had a clear view of them. He was not disposed to be objective about them, or to plumb the depths of that mysterious entity, character. He wanted only to assert the nature of the virtuous and the vicious, especially as seen in public men, in leaders.

And modern historians have not been kind to him either. They like to quote him on himself at the beginning of his life of Alexander: "My design is not to write history but lives." In Plutarch's time the word *biography* was waiting to be born, but his remark is still taken as proof that he was a biographer, not an historian.

The distinction is one that both historians and biographers like to make, and having Plutarch make it is of course pleasing to them. The trouble is that what he meant by it when he made it is not clear in context. It seems tacked on, an afterthought or an insufficient thought, something in answer to a question (or an accusation) we are not given. The life of Alexander itself is a loose chronological account of his exploits, and is not thesis-led, not an assessment mostly. It can easily qualify as history, excellent ancient history, among readers not troubled by boundaries. The obvious fact about it—and about Plutarchian lives even more sharply shaped by moral values—is that it straddles history and biography. In all his "lives" Plutarch was feeling his way into an art whose specifications he was not sure of; and at the moment of writing about Alexander he seems to have been in a limbo of his own making about the genre. The statement itself is a crux.

So, despite the statement, I make him my first biographer here, treating him as if he were father of the genre; but in doing so I know that I am neglecting earlier figures, such as Xenophon. I also recognize that I am neglecting a near contemporary of Plutarch's, the Roman biographer Suetonius. Suetonius was born thirty years later, and may well be the classical biographer most modern historians would choose over Plutarch. He was less committed to themes and dreams of virtue, and his relative modernity is attested to by Robert Graves, who did a fine translation of *The Twelve Caesars*. It is part of my thesis, however, that modern biographers have largely neglected the long and important tradition in biography of which Plutarch is the obvious early star, a tradition in which the shape of a written life was determined by something beyond chronology.

To many of us with little classical training, Plutarch's name first appeared in commentaries on Shakespeare's Roman plays. I can remember being dazzled by the discovery that one of the great passages in *Antony and Cleopatra* had been lifted, with iambic jugglery, straight out of Lord North's translation of a passage in Plutarch where Cleopatra took "her barge in the river of Cydnus, the poop wherof was of gold, the sailes of silver, which kept stroke in rowing after the sounds of the musicke of flutes" and many other instruments. (Shakespeare left out the other instruments.) Shakespeare was one of the world's great lifters, and he lifted more than a few bright passages. He lifted the narratives of his four Roman plays, plus a bit of *Midsummer Night's Dream*. Most important, he assumed Plutarch's ethical approach to character. Such lines as "This was the noblest Roman of them all," and "Then must you speak / Of one that loved not wisely but too well," may be mint Shakespeare, but they had deep roots in Plutarch's view of biography.

That view affected European literature for centuries. In a single tome, *The Lives of the Noble Grecians and Romans*, Plutarch handed down to future generations a definitive account of Greco-Roman standards for human conduct, together with rhetorical exhibits of how to express those standards. He may have had a greater impact on English drama than any Greek or Roman dramatist, and he was certainly the chief model, pagan or Christian, for the art of biography until modernity declared him to be no biographer at all.

He comes down to us, then, as a cultural phenomenon, first because of his rise to grace, and second because of his fall from it.

Time and place had something to do with his uniqueness. He had an advantage over his predecessors in that he was born at the moment of a great merging of the Greek and Roman cultures and grew up with the accumulated intellectual wealth of both. His father, a landowner in Boeotia (about a hundred miles from Athens), had managed to save his properties from the occupying Romans and had even learned to live amicably among them. Plutarch spent his childhood on his father's estate, then went to Athens to be trained by a philosopher named Ammonius. His philosophical bent gave him—though modern historians tend not to think so—still another advantage over his predecessors, for he was led by it to think of biography as more than just a subject for historians.

And to his philosophy he added training in rhetoric, which was standard in his time, though belittled by the philosophers. Thus Socrates was a great rhetorician but an effective opponent of rhetoricians, and Plutarch followed him in this, grounding his "lives" solidly in rhetoric while speaking out against it. Rhetoric did battle with philosophy, inside him, as a way to Truth.

He was also a student of natural history. His miscellaneous papers are full of sallies into the mysteries of nature: Why does the octopus change its color? Why are bees quicker to sting persons who have just committed an immoral sex act? Why does sea water not provide trees with nourishment? Where does the face in the moon come from? The spirit of inquiry was in him, though it was a muddled spirit. He was especially attracted to the unreliable medical lore of his time, and used it analogically to solve, he thought, many root problems of human conduct. For instance, he praised the Spartan lawmaker Lycurgus for doing for the Spartan state what "wise physicians do in the case of one who labours under a complication of diseases"—that is, "by force of medicine reduce and exhaust him, change his whole temperament, and then set him on a wholly new regimen of diet."

When Plutarch's father died he inherited the estate and, between extended trips to Egypt and Italy, settled upon it like a country squire—a Socratic one. Like Socrates, he was full of the love of good talk. He entertained constantly, and not too soberly, yet he liked to be uplifting and to give his guests topics for discussion. The results are still with us in the Loeb Classical Library—two volumes of "table talk." We do not know how much of the talk had a basis in real talk at

his table—what remains is artful and finished—but certainly the dialogues have the ring of the real. Even their subjects seem right for
drinking parties, if there must be subjects at all:

> Is philosophy a fitting topic of conversation at a dinner party?
> Why do men become hungrier in autumn?
> Concerning ivy: is its nature hot or cold?
> Why are women least liable to intoxication, and old men most
>   quickly liable?
> What is the most suitable time for coition?
> Why does the letter A come first?

Unlike the pattern for Socratic dialogues, the answers given at
these sessions were not regimented into being, step by logical step.
Several possible answers were put forth casually before the leader of
the discussion (not always Plutarch) issued the evening's definitive
solution, usually a reasonable compromise. In answer to the first
question above, for instance, philosophy was found to be fitting, so
long as it was not too philosophic.

He lived for a time in Rome and lectured on philosophy there, a
wise man well read in the available literatures. He became an honor-
ary Roman citizen, and filled his seventy years with significant public
service, including supervision of the affairs of the Delphic oracle. (He
was a priest, a sort of administrator; he tried to keep the place sol-
vent.) In the variety of his interests he was a Renaissance man before
the Renaissance, but the drift of his thought was steadily toward
ethics, and his ethics were those of an earnest public servant. When
he was not diverted from public issues by color changes in the octopus, he was busy writing on subjects like these:

> On the education of children
> Precepts for governing
> On virtue and vice
> How a flatterer may be distinguished from a friend

Yet there were odd excursions away from such high matter, including five short "love stories" that did not foster virtue and were
not romantic. They were full of rape and murder. They were stories
his later disciples wished to think were not his, not remembering that
all his famous "lives" were full of rape and murder too. The best
known of his lesser works is his attack on Herodotus, the good gray
Father of History. There is no doubt that Plutarch wrote it, but quite a

bit of doubt about what it tells us about him. In this text, titled "On the Malice of Herodotus," he does not sound like a patient Platonist at all, but is extremely malicious himself. Scholars have not explained why. Why did Plutarch become exercised about an historian born five hundred years before him? The best guess is that he had a closer target, a living historian perhaps, or a contemporary school of history committed to the kind of history—if one can define it—that Herodotus wrote. The tone of the piece was that of professional in-fighting, and the detail backing up his complaints was academic, oriented to the not-said or the undersaid. The only reason for his outburst that surfaced was his anger at the way Herodotus had described the homeland Greeks. Herodotus was an Asian Greek; Plutarch was a homeland patriot. So Plutarch sallied forth against an ancient belittler of Greek courage and integrity.

In his first sentence he doubted that Herodotus was honest. In the second he accused him of "supreme malice." In the third he announced that someone should expose him as a liar. Then for fifty pages he tried to expose him. He backed up his case with dozens of instances of what he thought to be prejudice against Spartans, Athenians, Thessalians, Boeotians—all Greeks west of the Hellespont. He wound up his polemic by asking if there were "anything glorious or great left to the Greeks." His conclusion:

> We must admit that Herodotus is an artist, that his history makes good reading, that there is charm and skill and grace in the narrative, and that he has told his story "as a bard tells a tale," I mean not with knowledge and wisdom but with "musical flowing words." To be sure, these writings charm and attract everyone, but we must be on guard against his slanders and ugly little lies which, like the rose-beetle, lurk beneath a smooth and soft exterior; we must not be tricked into accepting unworthy and false notions about the best and greatest cities and men of Greece.

So the good-natured host of relaxed table talk had a low boiling point. As the Loeb editors noted, this ending granted to Herodotus "the virtues of a lying poet, but not those of a historian." They might have added that, aside from the unexplained venom, the ending was the complaint of an historian. Wicked Herodotus had carefully culled his sources to make the worse cause appear to be the better one. He had damned with faint praise. He had deliberately omitted crucial evidence on the side of the homeland Greeks. And with calculated viciousness he had put his own slanted words into the mouths of others.

This last fault—giving words to the helpless dead that they might never have thought of themselves—was of course the common practice of ancient, lying poets, and lying dramatists too; and Plutarch himself practiced the art constantly. So why pick on Herodotus? The oracles of the time did not say, but if they had, they might have said he had been visited by a demon. He was at his worst in the episode.

Luckily, this malice is missing in his "lives." In them he was working within a form that asked of him that he be balanced, patriot or no; and balanced he was. His practice in them, when evidence was shaky, was to gather together several versions of an event, put them down for the reader's inspection, and then state his own preference—that, or find all the versions suspect. In the earliest "lives" (Theseus, Romulus, Lycurgus, Numa Pompilius) his sources were legends, most were written in verse, and he was appropriately doubtful of the lot. Of his research on Theseus he said that it was like exploring unknown territory on the edges of an old map. He did enjoy old maps, but he felt he had to apologize for enjoying them. After all, he was a philosopher-historian with higher standards for Truth than folklore; and so, he added, "Let us hope that Fable may, in what shall follow, so submit itself to the purifying processes of Reason as to take the character of exact history." And in the companion piece on Romulus he asked the reader to "receive with indulgence" such "stories of antiquity."

Plutarch had an antique side of his own, of course—his spurious medical lore. He thought that people grow tall when their "vital spirits, not being overburdened and oppressed with a too great quantity of nourishment . . . do, by their natural lightness, rise." He advised against procreation while in drink, "for those children that the parents beget may turn out to be drunkards." And he naturally shared with his culture a faith in the intimate daily interaction between heavenly and human order, as well as in the "humours" theory of human health and disease. He also accepted the practice of animal sacrifice as a way of penance and purification, and lived comfortably with the myths of the Greek and Roman gods, not rejecting the possibility, "though it be altogether hard to believe," that a divine spirit might so "apply itself to the nature of a woman, as to inbreed in her the first beginnings of generation." In other words, he was a man of his time. What was unusual about him was his relative skepticism, not his sometimes quaint credulity.

Among his primitive views, his addiction to rhetoric must be em-
phasized, rhetoric as a positive way to knowledge and grace, like philosophy. Though he put rhetoricians and lying poets into a common
circle in hell in several of his commentaries, he based his strategy of
comparison in the "lives" upon common rhetorical procedures. In
addition, a youthful speech of his, in praise of Alexander, must have
been largely a rhetorical exercise.

It was a proper tribute—fulsome, stagey, uncritical. It was presented as part of a debate and was aimed at rebutting a critic of Alexander who had declared Alexander's successes mere good fortune.
"No, no," cried Plutarch for a number of pages, "Fame and Grandeur
were dearly bought with the Price of his lost Blood, and many
Wounds. . . . His chiefest Guides and Counsels were Prudence,
Fortitude, Endurance and Steadiness of Mind." Plutarch even put
words in Alexander's mouth, saying to Fortune, "Envy not my
Virtue, nor go about to detract from my Honour," then listing a doz-
en of his exploits performed without Fortune's aid. As a clincher he
pointed to Alexander's genius for applying theory to practice as he
weaned conquered nations from "their former wild and savage
manner of living." Alexander's secret? "He was not a person that ever
wrote concerning arguments and syllogisms, or held disputes in the
Academy; for thus they circumscribe philosophy, who believe it to
consist in discoursing, not action."

The difference between this account and the one in Plutarch's
later life of Alexander was sharp. The life was almost devoid of judgment on the man. After writing the tribute, he may have decided that
Alexander had a few faults after all, or, more aptly, that encomia were
themselves faulty. Still, the exercise was a stepping stone to his later
balancings. Some scholars think that biography began with encomia,
and they are probably right. As a literary form it is an exercise in
extravagance, and thus necessarily suspect. Yet praise is not to be
scorned; the roots of poetry and of inspiration may be here.* The

---

* Not that the difference between *political* rhetoric and *divine* rhetoric was
ever easy to see. Shakespeare was an insistent clarifier here, obviously concerned
with the problem. Compare Antony's speech to the crowd in *Julius Caesar*, a
technical triumph only and one designed to make us see how unscrupulous he
was, with Portia's mercy speech in the *Merchant of Venice*. Portia's speech is a
technical triumph too, but it is also, in context, a divinely guided speech, comparable perhaps to "right reason" in Milton, of which one can be analytical and
critical, but there it is.

fervency of Plutarch's Alexander speech was probably genuine. Plutarch was young, an enthusiast, and from all evidence a true believer in divine guidance. He could say firmly, "To mix heaven and earth is ridiculous," yet he mixed them. He liked to set the two against each other, and then give the nod to heaven:

> This narrative [attributing divine guidance to Romulus and Remus in the founding of Rome] is suspected by some, because of its dramatic and fictitious appearance; but it would not wholly be disbelieved, if men would remember what a poet fortune sometimes shows herself, and consider that the Roman power would hardly have reached so high a pitch without a divinely ordered origin, attended with great and extraordinary circumstances.

◆ ◆

Fifty "lives" appear in the Dryden translation of Plutarch as edited in the nineteenth century by Arthur Hugh Clough. Of those fifty, forty are paired and compared, and two big ones—Alexander and Caesar—are conspicuously paired but not compared. Then there are eight unpaired lives in the volume that just seem out of place, not a part of the same project. Why, for instance, did he include the life of a Persian—Artaterxes—amid his Greeks and Romans? And why did he decide to include several partial lives, such as those of Galba and Otho?

Even omitting the eight out-of-place lives, Plutarch's collection comes to six or seven hundred thousand words. Plutarch wrote regularly and at large. He was not thwarted by having to research dozens of distinct subjects, all big. We do not know how much of his life was spent on them, or by what stages he chose his pairings, but the evidence we have tells us that at the outset he favored lawgivers, notably Lycurgus, Numa Pompilius, Solon, and Poplicola. At that time he seems to have thought he was embarked upon a philosophic study of government, something like Plato's *Republic*. Then he branched out, perhaps because he could not find many lawgivers with enough ideological sweep, and began to settle for powerful figures of any kind in the two cultures, so long as they had a bit of virtue hidden away somewhere. But the lawgivers, and especially Lycurgus, remained his favorites.

Lycurgus he presented as a leader who did everything right. He was diffident about accepting power, and gracious about releasing it. He read and profited by the *good* poets, notably Homer, and by philosophers who provided "serious lessons of state and rules of morality." He also traveled widely for instruction, observing the "sober and temperate" lives of the Cretans, and the manner by which the Egyptians separated the "soldiery from the rest of the nation." Most important, he sat at the feet of a great, wise man, Thales, who was a lyric poet, but who was also "one of the ablest lawgivers in the world." Thales' songs "were exhortations to obedience and concord" and "had so great an influence on the minds of listeners, that they were insensibly softened and civilized, insomuch that they renounced their private feuds and animosities, and were united in a common admiration of virtue." With this sterling background Lycurgus took over the commonwealth of Sparta.

Plutarch's account of Lycurgus codifying Spartan laws occupied three-fourths of his tribute to the man. It was framed by Lycurgus's birth and death, and followed by the life of a Roman equivalent, Numa. Then Plutarch compared Lycurgus and Numa in a separate rhetorical exercise—the pattern he would follow for most of his other "lives." It is a pattern that anyone who has taught *compare* and *contrast* in a classroom knows too well. The two lawmakers were alike, Plutarch said, in "their moderation, their religion, their capacity of government and discipline, and their both deriving their laws and constitution from the gods." They differed, he countered, in the governing problems they faced and in the legal steps they took to solve them. Numa formed a government "democratic and popular to the last extreme," while Lycurgus established the "rigid and aristocratical." Numa allowed "free scope in every means of obtaining wealth [except] military rapacity," while Lycurgus forbade "every form of moneymaking" and set up a kind of military commune. This listing of likenesses and differences was followed by an assessment of the relative success of the two men. In Plutarch's view, Lycurgus won with posterity: his legislation "continued above five hundred years," while Numa's "whole design and aim . . . vanished with him." Numa gained credits elsewhere, though. Plutarch had learned to be even-handed.

He then moved to Theseus and Romulus, a step backward in time that he must have taken after deciding that his collection of lives should be a chronological sweep of the Greek and Roman cultures.

Both men were so remote for him as to be nearer legend than history, and he was careful to suggest their remoteness by setting the many contradictory tales about them against one another. He also tried to make clear which of the stories he believed. He told, for instance, the tale of Theseus's affair with Ariadne (in which Ariadne stretched out a thread for Theseus that helped him find his way out of a labyrinth and slay a minotaur), and he added that "most of the ancient historians and poets agreed" on the truth of the tale—but he did not say that *he* agreed on it.

Also, in his life of Romulus, Plutarch complained (mildly) about the improbabilities that "fabulous writers" put forth in connecting Romulus's origins with divinity. And he doubted tales of the disappearance of Theseus and Romulus to the effect that they were not dead "but translated to a higher condition."

His doubts about what he knew of Theseus and Romulus did not keep him from comparing their characters, however. He found Theseus to be the more virtuous of the two (though a confirmed rapist, and probably the murderer of his father). He thought both men failed as rulers (though they were brave fighters). And he criticized both for letting themselves be governed by anger and jealousy. All in all, Theseus and Romulus came off poorly in his hands. He preferred that his heroes be more civilized than these two, civilized in the sense of working to consolidate and regularize their governance.

After putting Theseus and Romulus in place at the front chronologically, he was ready to move forward through his pairings, which can best be introduced in the accompanying chart.

Name	Date of death, B.C.	Primary roles	Primary qualities
Lycurgus	900?	lawgiver, disciplined socialist	rigid, temperate, self-sacrificing
Numa Pompilius	675	lawgiver, humane capitalist	relaxed, temperate
Solon	600	lawgiver; removed tyrant	both were public-spirited, philo-sophic, populist
Poplicola	503	lawgiver; removed tyrant	

Name	Date of death, B.C.	Primary roles	Primary qualities
Pericles	430	statesman-general	both were benevolent
Fabius	203	statesman-general	despots; Pericles was a "true Olympian"
Alcibiades	450	statesman-general	populist, intemperate, unscrupulous
Coriolanus	500?	general	patrician, temperate, proud
Timoleon	337	Greek leader of Sicily	gentle, open, unheroic
Paulus	160	Roman conqueror of Macedonia	stoic, noble, lofty
Pelopidas	364	statesman-general	both were fighters
Marcellus	208	statesman-general	"needlessly prodigal of their lives"
Aristides	470	statesman-general	liberal populist; penurious
Cato	150	statesman-general, writer	liberal populist; a sound economist
Philopoemen	184	statesman-general	great fighter; too ambitious
Flamininus	217	statesman-general	great fighter; obstinate
Lysander	395	statesman-admiral	moderate, persuasive, controlled
Sylla (Sulla)	78	dictator-general	ruled by force, but brave, public-spirited
Cimon	450	statesman-general	both were warriors
Lucullus	50	general-epicure	favored by the gods; Lucullus was in love with pomp
Nicias	413	statesman-general	noble loser, poor judge of character
Crassus	50	statesman-general	dishonorable loser; avaricious
Eumenes	316	statesman-general	shared common fate;

Name	Date of death, B.C.	Primary roles	Primary qualities
Sertorius	72	statesman-general	both oddly dispraised
Agesilaus	360	Spartan king	obstinate, malicious
Pompey	48	statesman-general	moderate; a friend-favorer
Alexander	323	conqueror	no assessment
Caesar	44	conqueror	no assessment
Phocion	317	statesman-general	both faced misfortune; because their virtue bore "the same colour, stamp, and character," they are not distinguishable
Cato the Younger	46	statesman-philosopher	
Demosthenes	322	statesman-orator	great speaker; modest, hard-working
Cicero	43	statesman-orator-writer	great speaker; boastful, good-natured
Agis	241	Spartan king	all were reformers who restricted patrician power; all were rash and inclined to despotism (Agis was Cleomene's uncle; the Gracchi were brothers)
Cleomenes	220	Spartan king	
Tiberius Gracchus	121	populist tribune	
Caius Gracchus	133	populist tribune	
Demetrius	283	statesman-general	both were "insolent in prosperity" and debauched, their bravery defeated by passion
Antony	30	statesman-general	
Dion	353	statesman, student of Plato	both were rebels against tyranny: Dion driven by self-interest; Brutus selfless
Brutus	40	statesman, idealist	

Note that the paired subjects were both culturally and chronolog-ically separate, being sometimes centuries apart. (The same principles applied today might pair Edmund Burke with William Jennings Bryan, or Oliver Cromwell with Lenin.) Note also that the leaders were usually paired because they had common functions in their re-spective societies, those functions being usually both military and political. And note most of all that qualities of character must also have figured in the choosing process. Plutarch did not pair two gener-als simply because they were generals.

One of the translators of Plutarch, Jacques Amyot,* said that Plu-tarch's ideal subjects were "men of high courage and wisdom, who . . . willingly yielded their lives to the service of the common weale, spent their goods, sustained infinite pains both of body and mind in defense of the oppressed, in making common buildings in establish-ing laws and governments, and in the finding out of arts and sciences necessary for the maintenance and ornament of man's life." He should have added that Plutarch did not find the ideal often or, after Lycurgus, expect to. Despite his critics' complaints, Plutarch knew, or at least came to know as he matured, what Plato meant when he said that great natures produce great vices, and that fact did not out-rage him. If it had, he could not have "done" Alcibiades or Coriola-nus. In no case, though, among the paired lives did he descend to minor figures. To include the undistinguished, he said, would have been like lavishing affection on "young puppy dogs and monkeys."

In the early lives he was content with pairings that did not produce a moral winner. (Lycurgus and Numa were equal in virtue, for in-stance, and were judged only by their long-term effectiveness as legis-lators.) But as he went on, the gamesman in him drove him, for a time, to choose moral favorites as if he were refereeing a game; and a game it was for him, a serious rhetorical game. He had no numerical rating system at hand like that at diving meets, but he managed to balance virtue and vice with great verbal precision, a precision that now seems, as the Loeb editors put it, artificial and forced:

> There is no dishonor in accepting a house and handsome estate [as Timoleon did]; but yet there is greater glory in a refusal. [Paulus was the refuser.]

* Amyot translated Plutarch into French. North's translation was based on Amyot's.

Pericles was a good prophet of bad success and Fabius was a bad prophet of success that was good.

To seek power by servility [Alcibiades] is a disgrace, but to maintain it by terror, violence and oppression is not a disgrace only, but an injustice [Coriolanus].

To conclude, since it does not appear to be easy, by any review or discussion, to establish the true difference of their merits [Philopoemen and Flaminius] and decide to which a preference is due, will it be an unfair award in the case, if we let the Greek bear away the crown for military conduct and warlike skill, and the Roman for justice and decency?

We are now qualified to consider whether we should go far from the truth or not in pronouncing that Sylla performed the more glorious deeds, but Lysander committed the fewer faults, as, likewise, by giving to one the preeminence for moderation, to the other for conduct and valour.

In his death Crassus had the advantage, as he did not surrender himself, nor submit to bondage . . . whereas Nicias enhanced the shame of his death by yielding himself up in the hope of a disgraceful and inglorious escape.

There was, of course, much similar balancing in Shakespeare, and the technique reached its climax—perhaps finale—in Samuel Johnson. But our culture has been inhospitable to it for some time. More pertinent is the fact that our culture has come to question the merit of trying to quantify abstract qualities. Plutarch must have done so too, for he later abandoned the practice; yet his commitment to it while writing most of the "lives" was clear and emphatic, showing his faith in the *solidity* of virtue—and vice.

The commitment also shows his faith in his age. Think of the intellectual enlightenment implicit in weighing, *precisely*, the justice, decency, and valor of his contestants. His optimism here is like the nineteenth century's faith in science and scientific progress, unwarranted but unbounded; and as with the nineteenth-century enthusiasts, it meant that he had to look down upon the unenlightened minds before his time, minds like those of the ancient lying poets.

He looked down on the poets just as Plato had, and he did so partly because they were writing in that primitive, irrational medium, verse. In an odd dialogue, "The Oracle at Delphi No Longer Given in

Verse," he presented his disputants as all equally patronizing to poets and in agreement that prose was a giant step forward.* Some poets were inspired, yes, and their ties to divinity were not to be scorned, but the disputants also hurried to grant that some had written dreadful hexameters. One of the debaters pointed out that the fault lay partly with the education of the sibyls, a typical sibyl being "inexperienced and uninformed about practically everything, a pure virgin soul who had become the associate of the God"; but their inexperience was as nothing beside their bad prosody. Their descent into prose—which must have occurred in Plutarch's own lifetime—was therefore a good thing, showing that the Greek language had at last "put off its finery" and was ready to go "on foot" in prose. It was ready to "sift" the true from the fabulous.

Plutarch's balancings were important ways of sifting. They were end products of the purifying processes of reason; and Plutarch's faith in them made the "sentencious" a science as well as an art. He used the word with approval, admiring those who had so purified their speech as to *achieve* sentenciousness, especially the Spartans, who were taught "to comprehend much matter of thought in a few words," and whose children, "by a habit of long silence, came to give just and sentencious answers."

A collection of sentencious sayings that Plutarch sent to the emperor Trajan was an ambitious case of purifying. He compiled it from his own "lives," and recommended it to the emperor as a collection of pearls for the busy executive who did not have time to read the "lives"; but he also said, in defense of the pearls, that "the true understanding of the characters and predilections of men in high places" was "better reflected in their words than in their actions." Was he being a sycophant, trying to sell the emperor his little guide to conduct? Possibly, but the process of purification or distillation is relied on too often in his work to be taken lightly:

> There is no use for bravery unless justice is also in evidence, and if all men should become just there would be no need for bravery.

> The Lacedomians above all others make it a practice to rule and be ruled.

* It was progress for the Darwins too. Erasmus Darwin wrote a treatise on plants in couplets, but Charles Darwin, though well read was strictly a prose man. He had advanced so far that he admitted he had trouble with Shakespeare.

Sayings like these are of a piece with the comparisons in the "lives," and while they now seem artificial and forced, they were at the fountainhead of knowing for Plutarch. Reason itself, he said, had chosen the art of comparison "expressly to choose and obtain some suitable, and to refuse and get rid of some unsuitable objects." He then described temperance, justice, and wisdom as arts of the same kind—in fact the supreme arts of the kind—since they were based in judgment and selection, and exercised not on the good and expedient only, but also on the wicked, unjust, and inexpedient. We have trouble following him here, but he was in good company. In the *Phaedrus* Socrates compared "the art of healing" with rhetoric, with the same emphasis on the probing nature of rhetorical action. "In both arts," he said, "you have to *analyze* a nature, in one the nature of the body, in the other the nature of the soul [italics added]."

If Plutarch were alive today in our country, he would find himself aligned on moral issues with persons who assume that virtue has no need of a critical intelligence—with Christian fundamentalists for instance, and with a variety of law-and-order groups who simply know what is right. He would have to remind them that he was a skeptical, critical pagan. His mistake, it now appears, was that he *advertised* himself as a moralist. The word sticks to him like a burr, and he is not allowed to have been an objective intelligence, not permitted to have been the rational student of character he thought he was. His mode of analysis may now appear defective, but it had its precisions, and it was also—once he moved beyond the encomium—a spacious mode, allowing him to admit all sorts of evidence to his cases, evidence that is now some of the best sociocultural history we have from his age. His lives of the early lawgivers are instances of his strength as a social historian, but he was also strong, though haphazard, on economic matters having to do with debts and the relationship of property ownership to human rights and political power. And as a source of information about the status of women in Greece and Rome, he is, though no advocate of equal rights, hard to beat. Unlike modern biographers, he had little liking for entering upon the private life—what the heroes ate for breakfast, how they dressed, and what they thought about when they were not plotting wars against the Persians—but he was a confirmed anecdotalist, so the private details crept in anyway. Today we learn more from the man when he was digressing than when he was on track.

Plutarch's life of Alcibiades especially shows his range. He is gossipy about Alcibiades' "friendship" with Socrates, and passes on details of his appearance (he was a great beauty, and he lisped) and of his exhibitionism (he stripped naked to be noticed, threw himself in front of chariots to make a point). As for Alcibiades' dress, Plutarch says that he wore "long purple robes like a woman, which dragged after him as he went through the market place." Of his eloquence, courage, and intelligence Plutarch makes much too, but he focuses mostly on the "exorbitant luxury and wantonness" of the man, without denying his greatness: "The force of his eloquence, the grace of his person, his strength of body, joined with his great courage and knowledge in military affairs," more than balancing his vices. He could be perfumed and in his cups, then visit the Spartans "wearing his hair close cut, bathing in cold water, eating coarse meal and dining on black broth." He could earn the people's love and their hate in a gesture. Both he and Coriolanus come off poorly in their virtue contest, but both survive the complaints, as Plutarch intended.

The life of Dion shows Plutarch's worldliness rather differently. Like Alcibiades, Dion was a member of the magic circle of Socrates and Plato, but upright, serious, and disciplined, a figure with the trappings of a philosopher king-to-be, Plutarch's ideal. The early pages of the life show this side of him and seem to be leading him to a career like that of Lycurgus, with high principles triumphant in government, and prudence and temperance triumphant in man. I came at Dion's life in ignorance, and knowing a little of Brutus, with whom he was being compared, I foresaw Dion as the easy winner between them, his principles *not* being flawed. Dion was "the quickest and aptest to learn" of Plato's students, and "the most prompt and eager to practise the lessons of virtue." He did not succumb to the bad influence of a governing tyrant (Dionysius of Syracuse), but instead led the tyrant himself toward virtue, even importing Plato in person to help him. And in the court of Dionysius he discoursed "so well of the present state of affairs that he made all the rest appear in their politics but children." He even showed himself to have, beyond his "passion for reason and philosophy," marks of greatness as a warrior. And being, besides all this, rich, he seemed a shoe-in. Then suddenly his fortunes as well as his virtues soured; his character grew tarnished by opulence and ambition. Brutus, that clear failure, got the nod.

In summary, then, most of the lives had a recognizable, repeatable structure (the exceptions being those of Caesar and Alexander, which I am about to describe): first, an opening generalization about the reliability of the sources used, about the subject's most conspicuous qualities, and perhaps the appropriateness of comparing him with the mate Plutarch had chosen for him; then a few facts of the early life, hastily disposed, with an anecdotal childhood event pointing to his particular *virtù*; then the career itself as general, consul, emperor, or whatever, developed in detail, with sometimes digressive comments about its effect on society; then the conclusion of the career, frequently abrupt, serving as a springboard to judgment of the man's success—which was not synonymous with his virtue, but close. This individual judgment led to a separate, detached section in which he was compared, in balanced phrases, with his mate.

But the long, long lives of Alexander and Caesar have no such transparent shape. They could well have been the ethical keystone of the whole immense collection, but they are not that. Plutarch had much to say about each, yet after the first sentence of the life of Alexander, in which he proposed "to write the lives of Alexander the king, *and* of Caesar, by whom Pompey was destroyed [italics added]," he made no gestures toward comparison, and only intermittent assessments of their actions individually. The shift was not, I think, for the better.

What was it a shift to? It was agreed "by all hands," he begins, that Alexander was descended from Hercules, and that some say his mother was visited by a god in the form of a serpent before his birth. He gives the exact day of the birth, and advises that "all the Eastern soothsayers" ran about "beating their faces, and crying that the day had brought forth something that would prove fatal to all Asia." He balances the mythic with incidental worldly matters—how Alexander bent his head, the color of his complexion—and seems to make his hero bigger than life, but a forked beast too. Thus Alexander tamed the untameable horse Bucephalus, and rode him for thirty years. Alexander had a falling out with his drunken father, and stood over him when he staggered and fell, saying, "See there the man who makes preparations to pass out of Europe into Asia, overturned in passing from one seat to another." Alexander took over the kingdom of Macedonia at his father's death (there is no further discussion of the father-son connection) and set out for Asia himself, via Thebes, where he enslaved thirty thousand, put six thousand to the sword, and then determined to be merciful. He terrified the Athenians but left them alive, then crossed the Hellespont with only 43,000 foot and 4,000 horse. He had with him only 70 talents for their pay (he was 200 talents in debt) and 30 days' provisions. In his first battle with Darius, the Persians lost 20,000 foot and 2,500 horse, while Alexander lost 9 foot and 25 horse. Sardis was then his, and the looting of Asia began (he sent home to his mother some "plate" and "purple garments"). He was now surrounded with great luxury, but remained by inclination Spartan except late at night. He exercised greatly, "and in marches that required no great haste he would practise shooting as he went along, or to mount a chariot and alight from it at full speed." He was temperate in his eating, less so in his drink. He liked to stay up all night drinking and boasting, then sleep through the next day before heading off to his next triumph. He beat Darius back beyond the Euphrates, and demolished him a third, or possibly fourth, time when he came at him "with a million of men." He was "proclaimed king of Asia," then invaded India and discoursed with Indian philosophers. He headed back through Persia, and Bucephalus died. He "put a whole nation to the sword" and began to be surrounded by ominous "prodigies." He became, suddenly, very superstitious and filled his court with diviners, whose gloom proved, as always, correct. He was poisoned (some affirm) by his old teacher Aristotle, with whom he had had a falling out.

The story of stories. But to what end? Let us turn to Caesar.

While still a boy, Caesar alarmed the consul Sylla with his ambition, but escaped, was taken prisoner by pirates, outwitted them, and had them all crucified. Then he was educated in statesmanship and oratory, but learned early to describe himself as a plain soldier given only to plain discourse. He had, according to Cicero, a "designing temper," and by spending lavishly among the people he became first an aedile, and then a high priest, thereby exciting in the senate and among the nobility "great alarm lest he now urge the people to even greater insolence." Cicero too was disturbed by him, and was tempted by, but declined, a chance to have him murdered. Caesar then became praetor, then was granted the province of Spain, then read of Alexander (the only cross-reference in the whole account), and wept to think that Alexander at Caesar's age "had conquered many nations." He rapidly became rich, did a bit of conquering around Spain, and returned to Rome to become consul (for the first time). He ran into more resistance from the patricians and appealed yet again to the people. With Pompey's help (Caesar's daughter had married Pompey) he received the governorship of Gaul and left off politicking long enough to become "not in the least inferior to any of the greatest and most admired of commanders who had ever appeared at the head of armies."

At the head of armies he captured 300 states in Gaul, together with three million men, and killed one million. (One army opposing him "did dissolve and vanish like a ghost or dream, the greatest part of them being killed on the spot.") He was an inspiration to his soldiers, yet not himself a great physical being, but a "spare man" with "soft white skin and distempered, subject to epilepsy." Yet he was spartan and athletic and "used war as the best physic against his indispositions," with "indefatigable journeyings, coarse diet, frequent lodging in the field, and continual laborious exercise." He was an expert rider, and would sit "with his hands joined together behind his back at full speed." He disciplined himself so far as to be able to dictate letters while riding. Following Gaul he moved on to Britain (with the conquest of which he might be said to have "carried the Roman Empire beyond the limits of the known world"), then back to Rome. He started a civil war with Pompey (signaled by his crossing of the Rubicon), and conducted himself to great battles in several countries, at last defeating Pompey in Thessaly. He then hastened to Egypt, where Cleopatra came to him in the night in a sack carried by a eunuch, and bore him a son, Caesarion.

Then off to Syria, Asia, Sicily, and at last back to Rome to become dictator. When Caesar decided that he should instead be king, the events dramatized by Shakespeare occurred. Caesar was ambushed and murdered. Almost as an afterthought Plutarch remarked at this point: "That empire and power which he had pursued through the whole course of his life with such hazard, he did at last encompass, but reaped no other fruits from it than the empty name and the invidious glory."

Was this remark meant to be a considerate judgment, from the evidence piled up, on the *character* of Caesar? It was, I believe, more nearly a commonplace on the ephemeral nature of greatness in general. What impresses me about Plutarch's handling of both Caesar and Alexander is how many golden likenesses and differences he, who had a passion for likenesses and differences, threw away: how Caesar rose to power the hard, political way, while Alexander fell into it by the death of his father; how Alexander performed his great warrior feats against foreign powers entirely, while Caesar divided his heroism equally between foreign and civil strife; how Caesar cut an even wider swath than Alexander, geographically; how secret and conniving Caesar was, compared to the open Alexander; how unsuited they both were for masculine physical triumphs (Alexander was little interested in women; Caesar was pale and epileptic); how they both moved their empires out to the edge of things; and how both were extremely cruel and bloody, though disposed to be, on occasion, for political reasons, merciful. It is not that I personally want to finish off these two lives *for* Plutarch, but that I wonder why he did not.

Or let me say that I did wonder, until I went through the motions of comparison that he must have gone through. Then I could see that a biographer could pile up likenesses and differences like cordwood, but say nothing that mattered much about either figure. With life stories like theirs, assessments simply could not be made central without frivolously belittling the history the life stories encompassed. One could not make a central issue, for instance, of whether Alexander and Caesar achieved "fame and grandeur" by luck or by "labour and indefatigable industry," since the central issue had to be the achieving itself. Their lives plunged along through their years with a momentum and significance one just recorded, then stood back from. The random immensity of history in their hands made the neatness of ethical biography inappropriate, inadequate, potentially a lie.

We know little about Plutarch's own life—much less about him than about his biographees. Apparently he did not conquer a single country, or tame a single wild horse. Apparently he was neither a great leader of men nor a great leader of thinkers. We are pretty sure that he was the author of most of the work that has come down to us as his, but of the order of composition we are less sure, and of his thoughts as he wrote we know nothing. We have no key to him other than that he was a patrician and seemingly upright in his conduct, in the way that he wanted all public servants to be upright. The range of his knowledge was great, but as he dabbled in everything and could be glib, it may seem greater than it was. The purity of his moral message was great too, but was it not sometimes hypocritical? What did he believe and what did he just say?

Sometimes he does seem a hypocrite. And a snob. Take the patronizing letter he wrote his wife upon the death of their fifth child. It is the only private document—if it was that—that has come down, but it sounds like a sermon. He had not even been on hand for the death or the funeral, and could have refrained—so a modern reader might mutter—from telling her how to conduct herself. Where was *he* in relation to the pieties he wrote her, telling her to be restrained in her grief, unostentatious, reserved? Was he alienated from her when he wrote, or merely male and lordly. Did he have any private life with her at all?

The same emptiness appears in his stated convictions about great men, and what made them great. He never explicitly veered far from his model, Lycurgus, who was able to pass on the golden precepts of his own private life of temperance, discipline, and justice to a whole nation. In his later "lives" Plutarch found no successor to Lycurgus nearly equal to him in virtue; and in his own worldly, Roman Empire life he could hardly have conducted himself like an ancient Spartan. So what do we do with his insistent Spartan model?

That model is of course a model of selflessness, a virtue admired down the ages until our own time. The capacity of Lycurgus for self-discipline, self-diminution, and self-sacrifice is not to be doubted, but what then did he have *for* a self? We go to the cupboard and the cupboard is bare.

We go to Plutarch's own cupboard and find it bare too. And in his analyses of the characters he undertook to describe, this bareness is always present, being relieved only by the ambiguous reportage of dreams. It was with dreams, omens, and divinations that Plutarch explored the inner recesses, finding there fears, premonitions, and doubt, or hope, assurance, and inspiration. Yet he did not think of the dreams as we do. He took them to be a kind of foreign presence, a something outside the self intruding upon the self. The self itself had to reckon with the presence, or take the problem presented by the presence to an oracle for interpretation; but it did not have to live with the presence, reckon with it as actually part of the self. The presence was an import.

So the self remained bare. And would stay that way until modern times. Plutarch, lacking a core for the self in dreams or in an inner thought-life, had as material for character analysis only his subjects' conduct. Conduct was what he could and did measure, not thought; conduct was the determinant. And because he was dealing with the great and the powerful, whose conduct affected the cultures in which they moved, his sallies into the genre of biography became, willy-nilly, sallies into history, whether he thought he was writing history or not.

He seems to have realized the inevitability of the conjunction when he came to write the lives of Alexander and Caesar. When he said of them at the outset that he was writing lives, not history, he was putting himself on the spot, and he must have realized as he went along that character merged with history in such cases. The self, whatever it was, became selfless not to be virtuous but because it could not help becoming so, being caught up completely in the sound-and-fury continuum it had in some measure created.

And with that discovery Plutarch was left without a genre, or without the one he had thought he had. The disciples who came after him would continue to look for virtue as the proper subject for biography, but Plutarch in his last years could not.

The shift in his thinking is evident not only in the Alexander and Caesar ventures, but also in the loose, *unpaired* lives of the collection as it has come down to us. There are only eight unpaired lives, and six of them seem to have had no pairing intent behind them, and to have involved no effort at making the isolate lives into models. The other two—those of Galba and Otho—appear to have been part of a wholly separate series of lives, the format of which is itself suggestive of Plutarch's change in thinking. This other series was of the lives of Roman emperors, chronologically rather than morally arranged, and from the evidence of Galba and Otho, not even thought of as biography. Galba was emperor in his old age for only two years (A.D. 68–69), and was succeeded by Otho, who reigned for just three months. Plutarch reported on the times of their reigns *only*; so his "lives" of them are really accounts of their terms in office. Of them Plutarch could not have said that he was not writing history, history of the most plodding, recorder variety.

More important, the accounts of Galba and Otho were history without eminent men at the center. With Galba and Otho, Plutarch moved away from great men to venal small-timers. The cupboard was bare of the heroic, Aristotelian models he needed, and of the principles of biography they fostered.

Plutarch will be remembered, though, as the prototype of ethical biography, and his late-life failures to separate biography from history are probably best thought of as evidence of biography's problem down the ages. What is biography anyway? Or what *can* it be? Even Plutarch did not know, and to his credit he—though a patrician grave spirit—*found out* that he did not.

II

Hagiography and Aelfric

In 1928 the historian and biographer Harold Nicolson became severe, and dismissed the trade of biography as 99 percent impure. As practiced before his own age, of course.

Impure was an odd word for him to choose, since the biographers he damned had for centuries been earnest purifiers, purifiers of humans. But Nicholson did not want pure humans. He wanted pure biography, pure in the quest for truth. He did not want biography to evade or suppress facts for "irrelevant considerations such as 'loyalty,' 'reverence,' and 'discretion.' " He wanted it to be "impartial and thorough."

The Victorians, those sufferers from modernity, were his main targets. His complaint about them was that they were too decorous to want truth. They winced at it. They could be depended on to think of "honest biography" as "crude and vulgar."

Eighteen hundred years earlier Plutarch had disposed of Herodotus for not being enamored of truth either, and he might have agreed with Nicholson about the Victorians; but he could not have gone much further with him. Too many centuries stood between them, centuries that actually changed the nature of the truth an honest quester might search out. Pontius Pilate is said to have asked the question, What is truth? and then to have refused to stay for an answer. He must have known that if he had stayed, he would have been trapped in an endless argument. It is not only that truth itself has proved to be a variable, but also that many kinds or levels of truth have battled to be the relevent, significant ones. There have been grave truths (and lies) and mean truths (and lies), and there has been much selectivity in the processing thereof. For behind the selecting there have been selves doing the selecting, selves with self-interests as well as their cultures' interests guiding them. The art of biography is not happy without selves, and the selves make Nicolson's plea for truth-purity idyllic.

The same is true of autobiography—truer, one might even say, impurely. Autobiography is a different subject and is not the central subject here, but it is certainly a related subject and a self-centered subject. Anyone writing about him- or herself is bound to be a truth-selector, and few who have done so have rushed to present themselves as irremediably mean. Saint Augustine (A.D. 354–430), in his *Confessions*—frequently cited as the first "true" autobiography—did not omit his own early meanness (though mostly he mentioned his sinfulness, a significant variant). Still, he was only a few pages into his life when the tributes began. Did it matter that he described his grave virtues as gifts of the Lord? Did it matter that he had learned "to delight in truth . . . hated to be deceived, had a vigorous memory, was gifted with speech, was soothed by friendship, [and] avoided pain, baseness, ignorance" by virtue of the fact that he had put himself in the hands of the Lord? From the point of view of a student of the genre, I think not. Whether provided by the Lord or by the saint, the truths about the saint were definitely selective, and the selections did not give us a *mean* saint.

Autobiography has also been more selective than biography in another sense. It does not give us, even now, the whole life chronologically. The death of heroes, and usually much more, is uniformly omitted, since authors cannot stand outside themselves and report.

How much, then, of a life report is enough to make it classifiable as autobiography? The disagreement among scholars is ludicrous, though admittedly brought about in part by the relatively recent coinage of the word itself. *Autobiography* seems to be a nineteenth-century word, and one scholar, John Morris, attributes its roots to the time when the Romantics fought off the Deists by asserting the reality of the inner life, the values of the self, the significance of the individual. Yes, but another scholar hurries us back to the early Egyptians and Babylonians to find the autobiographical germ *there* in the self-adulation of the mighty, who said such things about themselves as this:

No minor have I oppressed, no widow afflicted,
no peasant or shepherd evicted or driven away;
from no maste of five hands have I taken
his men for the corvee. No one suffered want
in my lifetime, no one went hungry in my day;
for when there was dearth I had all the fields
in the region tilled. . . . Thus I saved the
lives of the inhabitants. . . . I did not prefer
the great to the small in aught that I gave.
And when the inundations of the Nile were
abundant and the farmers rich in all things,
I did not impose a new tax upon the field.*

The religious faith of such potentates made a "confession" such as the above merely a form of self-justification before the gods, which was surely a selective business. The mightiest encomiasts of that period even went to the length of presenting appropriate deities with excellent autobiographical pictures of their state of earthly grace by erecting in their tombs complete stage sets of their lovely households. Still-life autobiography. No chronology.

For obvious reasons biography has trailed autobiography in self-centeredness, but it has been much influenced by autobiography, particularly when the persons written about have lived within the biographer's own culture and time. The hagiographers to be discussed here owed much to materials such as Augustine's *Confessions*. Similarly, the biographers of the classical cultures owed much to personal accounts, though the latter were vastly different. Thus Caesar's *Commentaries*, though written by the man himself, were characteristically in the third person and endlessly devoted to military campaigns. And the ostensibly private *Meditations* of Marcus Aurelius (A.D. 121–180) were private for the first chapter only. After that they were about men in general, good men, and how they should conduct themselves to *be* good. There was no chronology, no life story. Aurelius's classical self proved to be self-reticent.

Aurelius provides a particularly useful contrast to Augustine, not

* Georg Misch, in *A History of Autobiography in Antiquity*. Misch is also the source of the suggestion that elaborate early Egyptian tomb furnishings were a form of autobiography.

only because he lived two centuries earlier, but also because the two men were a religion apart; and at the core of their religious difference was the self, the "I." If Plutarch had been able to write a life of Marcus Aurelius, he might well have found in him a true model, like Lycurgus.

Aurelius's thoughts about service to society and the subordination of self have a Plutarchian ring throughout. They are grave, virtuous thoughts, but conspicuously unbiographical thoughts. They have won over many, many modern readers, as well as the publisher of Chicago's Great Books, but they manage to be quite unilluminating—one might even say deceiving—about the character of their author. Matthew Arnold just could not get over Aurelius's "charm, delicacy and virtue," and his capacity, rare among stoic Romans, to show his emotions. But one does not have to go far among those emotions in the *Meditations* to see their intent and drift: they were written for decorous public display. Unlike Augustine, who had at least to own up to his early sins to arrive at his purities, Aurelius was pure from the beginning. His grandfather, his mother, his relatives, his teachers, had all been outstanding models for him; and his father's meekness, constancy, dignity, modesty, cheerfulness, honesty, and accuracy also were models, such good models that Aurelius devoted four pages of praise to them without one word of complaint. (Could the father not at least have once drunk too much?) Even the gods had been kind to Aurelius, by providing him with such models and by seeing to it that he respected them. Plutarch would certainly have been tougher on Aurelius than Aurelius himself was, but Arnold was taken in.

In defense of Arnold I should say that other evidence not from Aurelius shows him to have been unusually dedicated to Roman ideals of service and selflessness, yet in the Arnold essay I am thinking of (it was made a preface to a popular edition of the *Meditations*), Arnold is so bowled over by Aurelius's manner and apparent moral delicacy that he agonizes for several pages about how Aurelius could possibly have been, as he was, a firm anti-Christian, and could have sent, as he did, a good number of Christians to their martyrdom. Arnold ended his agony by noting a vast cultural and religious difference between Christians and old Romans, but he failed to note the most obvious fact about the *Meditations*—that they were not really a self-accounting at all, but the presenting of a model. Much more directly than Plutarch, Aurelius was a public relations man for the classical ideals of discipline, moderation, uprightness, right-thinking, and avoidance of the trivial (to the classical mind most matters of self were at least officially trivial):

> See . . . in the whole connections of thy thoughts, that thou be careful to prevent what is idle and impertinent; but especially, whatsoever is curious and malicious [so that] if a man upon a sudden should ask thee, what it is that thou art now thinking, thou mayest answer This, and That, freely and boldly, that so by thy thoughts it may presently appear that in all thee is sincere and peaceable; as becometh one that is made for society, and regards not pleasures, nor gives way to any voluptuous imaginations at all.

What remarkable thought control! The passage may help explain how Aurelius could illogically insist, slightly later, that one should never be constrained either to dissemble or "to lust after anything that requireth the secret of walls or veils." He had his id in a stockade.

Plutarch would have approved. They were both insistent purifiers of the beast in man. So of course was Augustine, who fought the beast in Augustine for hundreds of pages, but it was always clearly Augustine's beast he was fighting. He was attentive to his own "I," of which he spoke often—so often that a stoic Roman would probably have been annoyed and contemptuous. Aurelius, when he spoke of the beast, did it like this:

> To be capable of fancies and imaginations is common to man and beast. To be violently drawn and moved by the lusts and desires of the soul, is proper to wild beasts and monsters, such as Phalaris and Nero were. To follow reason . . . and not to trouble and molest that spirit which is seated in the temple of his own breast . . . but to keep him propitious and to obey him as a god, never either speaking anything contrary to truth, or doing anything contrary to justice, is the only true property of the good man.

Those are pieties, grave affirmations of worthy qualities, but as self-truths they are nothing, nor were they meant to be. They have been laundered. Augustine also was a launderer, but he traveled a different route entirely. He did not leave himself out when considering the lusts in need of laundering:

> To Carthage I came, where there sang all around me in my ears a cauldron of unholy loves. . . . To love then, and to be beloved, was

sweet to me; but more, when I obtained, to enjoy the person I loved. I defiled, therefore, the spring of friendship with the filth of concupiscence, and I beclouded its brightness with the hell of lustfulness; and thus foul and unseemly I would fain, through exceeding vanity, be fine and courtly.

Nor did Augustine suggest that he could have controlled lust by reason; it was the Lord who had to lead him out of his foulness.

Oddly, though, Aurelius did not think he could control lust by reason alone either, and he acknowledged that his villains, Phalaris and Nero, had been reasoners. He left the control to what sounds like the individual conscience—"that spirit which simply is seated in the temple" of the breast. That spirit was merely less individual in Aurelius, more social, more an establishment spirit, than Augustine's.

For Aurelius and Plutarch were indeed from a different world than Augustine. Plutarch was a rich, gregarious, patrician citizen of the Roman Empire; an habitué of Athens, Alexandria, Rome; an insider known to emperors. Marcus Aurelius was even richer, more worldly, more patrician, more everything, being himself an emperor. In contrast Augustine, though an intellectual, was middle class (his father was a burgess in a North African town, the one later named after Constantine), and thoroughly removed from the Empire machinery that created, for noble Romans, their official conscience.

And the monks before and after Augustine whom we call the hagiographers were further removed. Surrounded by a rapidly growing monastic system, they were committed to an ascetic, outsider's life, and the commitment quite separated them from emperors, generals, court annalists, and the like, thereby limiting the range of their scholarship and their views. Having been persecuted, ostracized, and only slowly accepted, they could not ooze decorous gentility as a virtue even if they wanted to, or go to the palace and talk with other worldly ones. They traveled a good deal, but traveled within the growing, culturally restrictive Church system. They would have known even less than Augustine what Aurelius or Plutarch thought the self was, or where it resided.

Indeed, the ignorance of most early Christians about the great heritage of Greece and Rome was one of the conspicuous manifestations—almost as conspicuous as the fall of the Empire itself—of the cultural throwback we call the Dark Ages. Accordingly, the hagiographers' notion of the proper ingredients of a self—and *how* the truth of a self was to be laundered—was much more foreign to the virtue-notions of Plutarch and Aurelius than might first appear.

The sources of this foreignness were the legal and cultural dimensions of the Christian Gospel itself. Jesus was legally accused of blasphemy and insurrection, and the reasons for these accusations are a complicated part of Church history that is relevant here and that I, though a fallen Christian, must try to sum up.

The Old Testament can be looked at as a tribal chronicle becoming a national chronicle, yet not losing the tribal feature of familial, ethnic bonds. Within that chronicle many biographies were embedded—most notably those of Moses and Joseph, being long and detailed—and these lives were among the precursors of Greek and Roman biographies, such as Plutarch's. In both cases the individual lives were wholly bound up in their cultures' laws and officialdom, though in Plutarch's case the author was not a scribe in the old sense of "official reporter."

Then came Christianity, whose early relationship to officialdom was that of a counterculture. The New Testament, as well as the biographies that were embedded in it and succeeded it, received their thematic drive from being opposed to officialdom. As far as biography was concerned, the injunction "Give unto Caesar the things that are Caesar's" was changed to read "Give unto Caesar the biographies that are Caesarly," with the addendum "We will do our own." For in its beginnings Christianity was neither tribal nor national but—there seems to be no other word—spiritual, and the biographical genre it encouraged was therefore not of the world of chronicle.

The difference may be said to have begun with the difference between Moses and Christ. Moses was an official lawgiver to his tribe-nation, while Jesus was an opponent of both Jewish and Roman law. Jesus' history is so cleanly that of the outsider that we can perhaps learn more from his follower Paul (in Acts and in his Letters to the Romans and the Corinthians), who was converted to Christianity from the doctrines of two cultures, and provided much detail of the legal, formal difficulties.

Proselytizer Paul had a thoroughly legal mind. He said himself that as a Jew he was among those who spoke and acted against the Christians for their violations of Jewish law, before Christ came to him on the road to Damascus and converted him. Finding himself, then, on the other side of the law, he was well equipped to speak of its limitations, and did. He was also a Roman citizen, ready to cope with Roman law, use it, and find refuge in its relative freedoms from the harsh response of the Jews to his campaigning. The last part of Acts is a kind of biography of Paul's activities as he escaped flogging (and worse) from the Jews by appealing to an ascending series of Roman courts. And his letters tell us what he must have told those courts.

He preached that Christians reached for a righteousness based on faith, while the Jews lay claim to a righteousness of law. He said that Christians had determined to "adapt" themselves "no longer to the pattern of this present world," and that in cases of dispute they were to take their problems "to the community of God's people" rather than "pagan law courts," not trusting "jurisdiction to outsiders." He said that if a slave were called to Christ, and "a chance of liberty should come," the slave should "take it." He said that circumcision was "neither here nor there," legally or spiritually. He recommended to "those Gentiles who are turning to God" that they "abstain from things polluted by contact with idols." And so on. He was in effect a steady advocate of civil disobedience to tribe or nation, angering the Jews but finding among the Romans mixed tolerance upward to the judgment of Caesar himself, at which point the story stops.

Reading Acts is a little like being deprived of the last installment of a movie serial, but the enduring outcome of the meeting of Paul and Caesar, if they met, seems clear enough. Paul's case simply was not solved then. It raised an issue that was to be resolved first one way and then another within the Empire, up to the time of Constantine. At root the issue was whether or not a self had legal rights *as* a self, an independent being.

And the case raised another issue of self that went beyond law and was never solved at all. How could the things that were Caesar's be separated, *within* a self, from the things that were not? How could a self throw the world away and at the same time fight the good fight for worldly victories? With Paul's kind of encouragement, the martyrs of whom the hagiographers came to write were uniformly powerful, self-willed persons who went forth to mortal combat with the world. Though they could argue—as did T. S. Eliot's Becket before his murder—that they avoided the "higher vice" of self-will by letting God's will do their willing, their pieties here seem, to a religious skeptic, overly wrought. (So, sometimes, do Eliot's own.)

And certainly we cannot let these martyrs off this hook by calling them lacking in self-awareness. Did they not ring all the changes of

self, from fierce self-denial to equally fierce self-glorification? Aware
of self they surely were, obsessed with self they surely were, though
they did not use such words as ego and id.

It must be granted, though, that among the early Christian monks
who recorded the martyrs' actions, such awareness was not usually
cultured or complex, like Paul's. Reason did not thrive among them,
nor did sound reporting or scholarship. In the tombs and mountains
of Egypt, Saint Anthony (ca. A.D. 250), for instance, needed no books
or courses in logic to help him talk with demons and angels, and when
he did so he observed no shadings of black and white. Note in the
following passage—reported by Anthony's contemporary and biographer, Athanasius, a learned exception within the fold—how Anthony puts down the Greeks for their studiousness (he is speaking to
disciples who have come to the mountains to learn from him):

> Virtue is not far from us, nor its home apart from us. No, the thing is
> within us, and its accomplishment is easy if we but have the will.
> Greeks go abroad and cross the sea and study letters, but we have no
> need to go abroad for the Kingdom of Heaven, nor to cross the sea to
> obtain virtue. The Lord has told us in advance the Kingdom of
> Heaven is within us.

If such words were spoken in a modern context, we would assume
their figurative element to be large, but with Anthony the figurative
seems not to have been separable from that which it figured. Though
the kingdom of heaven was within, it was not thereby a mere fancy.
Not the self, but the Lord, had put the kingdom there, and that was
that.

It was the cultured Athanasius (whom Cardinal Newman praised,
in the late nineteenth century, for his learned arguments against Ar-
ianism), and not Anthony, who was worldly about spiritual kingdoms, and aware of the tricks of the figurative. He dutifully passed on
Anthony's message of simple ascetic faith, but like a few other early
figures in the Church with classical educations, such as Saint Benedict
and Saint Basil, he was not himself a simple ascetic. Nor was his life of
Anthony simplistic. If it had been emulated by later hagiographers,
the genre would have been altered—for the better.

Athanasius described, for instance, Anthony's adolescent with-
drawal from the haunts of men with sufficient specificity to interest a
modern psychiatrist. It seems that Anthony was about eighteen when
his parents died and he began to receive visitations in the form of little

beasts and black spirits. One particular black spirit was the spirit of fornication. Anthony fought him off, and then contended with many nightmarish animals, all of which Athanasius presented as clearly products of Anthony's own mental life. Inner life had not been Plutarch's subject—he had written of dreams as incursions, somehow, from outside—and it would not be the subject, in any realistically reportorial sense, of later hagiographers. Yet Athanasius made it the core of his biography of Anthony. Though he did not speculate in a modern way about Anthony's obvious problems with his animal, sexual self, he did report physical oddities: that Anthony was never known to have removed his clothes before any other person, that he never washed, and that he was said to have performed a true miracle of inhibition—that of fording a stream without removing his clothes or getting wet. In the long history of purification rites, pagan and Christian, few insiders have approached the rites except as untouchably spiritual events, but Athanasius did. His life of Anthony was an early Christian model that no one followed.

The model was definitely not Saint Adamnan's (A.D. 624–704) in far-off Ireland, when he wrote his biography of Saint Columba (A.D. 521–597). Ireland's early monastic history was distinctly separatist, and while it developed comfortable communal arrangements (bringing nuns and monks together in common enterprise), it also bred a provincial state of mind, one that found it appropriate to elevate and purify the spiritual life by omitting the physical life, or denying its meanness. Adamnan's physical account of Columba was limited to recording that "he never could spend the space of even one hour without study, or prayer, or writing, or some other holy occupation"; that from boyhood he was "brought up in Christian training and the study of wisdom"; and that he "so preserved the integrity of his body and the purity of his soul, that though dwelling on earth he appeared to live like the saints in heaven."

In such descriptions the principle of the eulogy was operative, leaving Columba with no faults, with no struggles even, no wrestlings with demons. He was wholly at peace, ready for heaven, and after the paragraph from which I have quoted, Adamnan was ready to take him there. For one hundred pages he then scorned to report any details of what we would call the life, instead citing unlocalized miracles taking place "at one time" and then "at another time" in Columba's unearthly career. Columba had only to pray and bothersome wild boars stopped being bothersome; fatal sicknesses in passers-by vanished;

inconveniently heavy stones consented to float; broken bones were healed; demon-polluted wells were purified. And Adamnan, dutifully putting such wonders down on paper, was so convinced of their literal verity that he bragged of his scholarship in discovering them:

> Let no one think of me as either stating what is not true regarding so great a man, or recording anything doubtful or uncertain. Let him know that I will tell with all candor and without any ambiguity what I have learned from the consistent narrative of my predecessors, trustworthy and discerning men, and that my narrative is founded either on written authorities anterior to my own times, or on what I have myself heard from some learned and faithful ancients, unhesitatingly telling facts the truth of which they had themselves inquired into.

Reading that, one might even think that Adamnan had been reading Harold Nicolson, yet the man had to be sincere. Truth in Ireland in the sixth century was like that.

So the hagiographers were a very mixed breed, with Athanasius at one end of the spectrum and Adamnan at the other.* The Benedictine monk Aelfric, coming somewhat later (A.D. 955?–1020) was somewhere in between.

◆ ◆

In about A.D. 1000 Aelfric, about to become an abbot and to preside over an abbey in Dorsetshire, composed homilies, or sermons, on the lives of some twenty-five saints. The number did not equal that of Plutarch's noble "lives," but it put Aelfric in Plutarch's league. Aelfric's inclusiveness also did for Britain what at the time badly needed to be done. It took Christian history back to the martyrly origins of sainthood.

Doing this was not quite equal to Plutarch's revival of the legends of Theseus and Romulus, but it came close. Aelfric not only had no

---

* Adamnan seems to have been a devout primitive whose motives in writing Saint Columba's life were a missionary's. Later in the history of hagiography we find suspiciously mercantile exploitation of the credulity of medieval Europe generally. One book, *Legenda Aurea* [The Golden Legend], by Jacobus de Varagine, was a great compilation of saintly miracles whose compiler made no effort whatsoever to assess his sources. It was an immensely popular book; five hundred copies of the manuscript are said to be extant, and when books began to be printed, it went through 150 editions. So say the modern publishers, not mentioning the author's motives.

personal knowledge of the ancient martyrs (ca. A.D. 250–350) but also had no way of assessing the value of his sources for their biographies. Nor did he brag about the value of his sources, but instead spoke modestly of the plebeian, unscholarly character of his whole project. He seems to have been a true scholar like Athanasius, though without Athanasius's access to great libraries.

What Aelfric had behind him, one century back, was the great King Alfred, who had himself been a busy translator of a few ancients, preferably Christian, into Anglo-Saxon. Alfred was never so tied up fighting Vikings that he did not have scholars around him reading him holy texts. For him a scholar was like a talented professional ball player in our culture, and when Asser, his future biographer, came into his life, he gave the man two complete monasteries, "as well as an extremely valuable silk coat and a quantity of incense weighing as much as a stout man," to keep Asser from returning to his native country.

Naturally Asser stayed, and before long, "all on one and the same day," Alfred began "through divine inspiration to read Latin and to translate at the same time." His new learning led him to translating—freely—passages he liked, and putting them into a handbook "he conscientiously kept to hand by day and night." Alfred himself described his mode of translation as analogous to collecting wood in the forest, and recommended to others that they not try to bring in great stocks of wood, but that "each load his wagon with fair twigs." Aelfric in turn, as will be seen, brought fair twigs to his fellow monks and the commoners, following Alfred's lead.

And Aelfric and his fellow monks were much indebted to Alfred for making England habitable for monks. Alfred was an excellent raiser of taxes, and he divided his revenues, in accordance with a passage he had translated from the Bible, into two parts, with one part going to his thanes and fighting men, and the other—"marked out for God in full devotion"—to monasteries, churches, and schools. Further, he saw to it that his thanes took to learning, threatening them with loss of secular powers if they "neglected the study and application of wisdom." As a result, Aelfric was educated in the shelter of a benevolent, learned thane by the name of Aethelmaer, as well as a scholarly Benedictine officialdom, and very early Aelfric's superiors seem to have agreed that his duty, as well as theirs, was a missionary one, that of bringing the message of Christ to those who could not—and even most of the monks of that time could not—read Latin.

Aelfric became a tireless translator of the writings of many Christian ancients, but he practiced, as Aelfric scholar Walter Skeat put it, "the principle of omission." It had been Alfred's principle with the twigs from the forest—do not bring them *all* home—but Aelfric practiced it to meet his own missionary purpose. He was an activist, an uplifter. Skeat, the busiest modern medievalist of all, has described him as "one born to be a teacher, who simply strove, with unflagging industry, to do his duty in instructing men in all such truth as he believed to be for their profit." Skeat in his long career took on not only Aelfric but also Chaucer and half the writers of the Middle Ages, and found Aelfric to be a man "of humble, upright and honest heart"; but he did feel impelled to mention Aelfric's attention to *profitable* truth. He also added this: "Avoiding heresies and superstitions, he set before his readers many valuable and primary truths, in so far as the learning and spirit of his age enabled him to do."

Skeat may have been too kind. About the Scriptures Aelfric was a literalist and seems to have believed anything he read. Yet the literalism *was* part of "the learning and spirit of his time," and certainly Skeat was right to sympathize with him for the cultural box he was in, and to praise his simple eloquence as he molded the genre of biography—the little piece of it that entered his world—to his missionary duty of loading the laic wagons with fair twigs.

Aelfric's fair twigs were saintly models. He would have agreed with Plutarch that seeing "moral good inspires an impulse to practice," but the moral good of the models he chose was founded on conversion to Christ, with its attendant social and spiritual shocks. None of Plutarch's noble Greeks and Romans had ever experienced conversion, or dealt with it as a force around them. Religious and ideological dissent had not been a serious factor in their dozens of wars, and I believe that Plutarch never had to confront a biographee who rejected, morally, the whole government establishment he worked and fought for. Nowhere among Plutarch's "lives" is there a figure who suffers a sea change such as that signified by conversion.*

And given Plutarch's dedication to state service, it seems likely that if there had been one, Plutarch would have dismissed him as a traitor.

---

* Coriolanus does not count. In Plutarch's opinion, his problem was not one of political or religious difference with Rome, but "ungraciousness, pride and oligarchical haughtiness."

Yet, for Aelfric, conversion was the point at which any story of virtuous conduct had to begin, preferably conversion resulting in martyrdom. In the period before Constantine the main narrative components of a saint's life, as passed down to Aelfric, were these: birth to a pagan family (or at least birth within an anti-Christian community); conversion, baptismal vows of chastity; a battle with tempters in a hostile environment; dissemination of the Word in a hostile environment; confirmation of the saint's sanctity by heavenly signs; heaven-led acts leading to the defeat or conversion of some Roman authorities; a martyr's death accompanied by instant ascension to heaven. For Plutarch, all of this would of course have been of the order of legendary matter.

It would also have been unfamiliar matter, alien matter.

It was alien matter in some respects for Aelfric's people too. Certainly Aelfric approached them with it as if it were. (Plutarch on the other hand had been constantly referential, assuming considerable knowledge of Greek and Roman history in his readers.) Aelfric was a persistent elucidator and simplifier. When he had a biblical passage before him he could not let it go. Thus, of the beginning in Genesis, he wrote in one of his homilies:

> Here you may hear that the heavens did not exist formerly, before the almighty made it in the beginning, and all the earth, by his skill. But he himself, who so mightily made such skill, was ever a creator without beginning.

Nor was that enough. He had also to chastise any listener, like Plutarch perhaps, who was skeptical:

> Very foolish is the man, and deceived by the devil, who is unwilling to believe that the living God was always in existence before he formed the creatures.

The pedagogue in Aelfric led him to compose his "lives" for Sunday use (he even provided appropriate dates for each homily), and the demands of the homily form in turn led him to the "principle of omission" mentioned above. He streamlined and simplified the narrative of each life to fit an instructive hour or two (their lengths varied considerably), and while he did not, like later divines, provide an opening biblical text for which a life would be illustrative, such texts were only an inch below the surface. Each life was present to give particularity and substance to the themes of conversion, martyrdom, and salvation. Each life was thus in the Lord's service, and saints were simply saints, devils devils, as in the later morality plays. Here is Saint Agnes, for instance, berating a young tempter as if on stage:

> Depart from me, thou fuel of sin, food of crime, and nourishment of death, depart from me! I have another lover. . . . From his mouth I have received milk and honey; now already I am embraced by his pure arms.

On the other side of the stage the father of the tempter then defends his son:

> Thou cruelest woman, wouldst thou show
> thy fiendlike sorcery, to destroy my son?

Aelfric was definitely keeping the congregation awake with such lines, and scholars defending his simplicities keep pointing to the credulity of his audience. But what of his own convictions? The best evidence is that he really believed in his simplicities, believed in miracles, believed in the purity of the loves he described and their heavenly reward—yet the best evidence is not very good. It glosses over the nature of his own life, since in his cultural climate faith was a group venture, not something to be questioned. He and his fellow monks, as well as those he proselytized, joined the heavenly host by matching with their own faith the faith of their martyred predecessors, and in doing so they abandoned private perceptions, convictions, doubts.

The abandonment was momentous, especially for the health of biography, and a skeptical mind like mine keeps having Harold Nicolson's craving for truth. My own constant problem is that of trying to mediate between the literal and the figurative in Aelfric's "lives," since the two continually merged. There was, for instance, the fabulous life of Saint George, prefaced by a remark (probably carried over by Aelfric in translation from his source) that heretics had "written falsehoods in their books" about him. What could the falsehoods possibly have been beyond those that Aelfric then propagated? He said that George was a "rich noble under the cruel emperor Datian" who, seeing the "error of the heathen," offended that "fiendish" emperor. The emperor called his magician to take care of George. The magician tried two deadly poisons on George. The poisons did not work and the magician was himself converted to Christ by George. "Then Datian became fiendishly angry" and had his magician beheaded, and had George bound to a wheel; but with George on the wheel the wheel "burst asunder," so that Datian had recourse to boiling lead. It cooled. At last Datian managed to burn George alive, but even as he did so and was on his way home—a fine detail—he was himself slain by fire from heaven. He went to hell at that time, while the "holy George journeyed to Christ, with whom he dwelleth in glory."

Reading of Saint George I was chiefly struck by the physicality of the action, including the final descent and ascent. Both the bad emperor and the saint headed off into the afterlife as if on a walking tour. How odd that purification should take such a turn.

My problem intensified with Saint Julian and his wife, Basilissa, a fable in which Julian took "a mate for himself who would not sever him from his pure life." Jesus prepared this match by speaking to Julian in a dream, saying that he and his maiden would, if they remained pure, be received in heaven. Waking, Julian went out and found himself a pure maid, married her, "and then the two came into one bed together." Julian then prayed to Christ, the bed was filled with the fragrance of roses, and Basilissa wondered at the fragrance until Julian explained. "This fragrance," he said, "is from Christ who is a lover of purity. If we two continue in unbroken chastity, and purely love him, then shall we come to His kingdom." Naturally Basilissa replied that she desired "to continue in pure maidenhood . . . so as to have life eternal, and the Saviour for her bridegroom," at which point the bridal bed "shook, and a bright light shone there, and Christ was visible." Soon the two of them were predictably persecuted by "the bloodthirsty emperor who was named Diocletian," but the predictable result, salvation, came quickly. From this tale I came away wondering where to locate the beginning and end of the "dream"—an irrelevant cavil, but my own.

But in sharp contrast there was Saint Mary of Egypt, who for pages and pages confessed (to an abbot, Zosima) to her "subjection to sinful lusts." She took no money for her "unlawful burning," but continued in her vile ways for seventeen years, satisfying her "culpable desires for wicked living" with hundreds. At last she entered the vestibule of a temple, where "a knowledge of salvation touched [her] mind and the eyes of [her] heart," and from that moment she was on the mend, being soon purified forever in the river Jordan without even the intervention of a fiendish emperor.

With Saint Mary I was crudely left wondering about the seventeen years of her not asking for money for her satisfactions. Was it that not taking money was somehow a purer form of lust to repent of? Or was the narrator merely adding realistic detail? I also pondered inconclusively the sermoner's delectable lingering over Mary's limitless frailty, but finally decided I was just not supposed to worry about him or her. Enjoy! the good monk Aelfric seemed to be saying of her, as Chaucer might have.

The good monk himself called his "lives" translations, but the scholars have quibbled about the word, noting his mixed respect for, and doubt about, his sources, as well as his freedom with them. A characteristic conclusion is John Pope's: "His work approaches original composition, not merely in style . . . but even in substance. . . . the thought is scrupulously traditional yet fully digested and feelingly his own." What that conclusion misses is that Aelfric did not think of his work as his own. His most conscious contribution to the "lives" was of the order of verbal embellishment to fit a sermon format. Embellishment was dear to Aelfric. He worked hard at giving his sentences clarity, balance, finish. He experimented constantly, and came to favor a loose alliterative verse that Pope, whose studies of the verse are extremely detailed, has decided should be called instead rhythmic prose (lest Aelfric be accused of writing bad verse). Prose or verse, it was an expressive mode that he liked and lavished his energies on.

The language and tone of the homilies roamed between the solemn and the luscious, both being appropriate for sermons. First, as Pope observes, there were the balancings suitable for "grand truths," producing "a solemn and incantatory" tone. I suppose the passage about Genesis already quoted (page 48) is typical. Note how the verse lines of the last part of the passage are halved, and set against each other (my small translation effort here is simply to show the balance):

A fool is the man   and by devils bedazzled
if he cannot perceive   that the all-living God
had being eternal   e'er creating his creatures.

Second, there was the narrative and dramatic mode, for which Aelfric employed unevenly long, flowing, unbroken lines:

Then said Lucy, "listen to my counsel;
thou canst take away nothing with thee
    out of this life,

and that which thou wilt give at death
　　for the lord's name,
thou wilt give because thou canst not take it
　　away with thee."

Sometimes the words were monosyllabic and unadjectival, and sometimes they were extravagant, as in this passage about Saint Agnes and her tempter:

I have another lover, unlike to thee in nobility,
who hath offered me better adornments,
and hath adorned me with unimaginable honor.
He hath encircled my right hand and also my neck
with precious stones, and with shining gems.
He hath set his token upon my face,
that I should love none other beside him.
He hath decked me with a robe woven of gold. . . .

There is nothing primitive about the prosody here. It is flexible, easy, functional, a clear sign of Aelfric's sophistication as an embellisher. The primitive in Aelfric was separate from that. It was the collective primitive in which his life was immersed, the before-writing part of him. At his desk, facing the immediacies of composition, he was a mature artist.

Nowhere was the embellishment process more pronounced than in his descriptions of the purity achieved by the saints. Except for Saint Mary, they were virgins all. The rivalry that Athanasius had spoken of centuries earlier, between monks competing for prizes in asceticism, carried over to the saints themselves, and Aelfric was always happy to give play to their furious antisexuality. He could even make a little pulpit drama of the antagonism between competing virgins, pagan and Christian. Thus the father of Saint Agnes's young tempter was the wicked prefect Sempronius, who, hearing of Agnes's rejection of his son's advances, was angered and told Agnes that she would have to be—since she chose to be virginal—a *Vestal* virgin; that or "be associated / with foul harlots and foully dishonored." Agnes replied "with great resolution" that she despised his threatenings and would have no traffic with the goddess Vesta. A more detached biographer would perhaps have questioned the difference between Vestal and Christian purity, but for Aelfric there was no reason to reflect. He sent Agnes right off to the harlots, where, far from being dishonored, she quickly purified their whole establishment.* For Aelfric the basic narrative drift was as inviolable as the saints themselves, leaving him, as an innovator in the genre, with only the lesser elements of his "lives" to improvise.†

Noting this, a modern skeptic must of course keep saying with Harold Nicolson that the trouble with Aelfric was that his own limits, or his culture's, kept him from participating in the great truth-search.

---

* For the Romans, Vesta and her virgins were the protectors of the home and, by extension, the state and the powers of the state. Christian virgins were something of the same for the counterculture.

† Not all the saints' lives recorded in the Middle Ages were so limited, though to describe the range of hagiography would be a large, and ecclesiastical, undertaking. For instance, in a life of Saint Odo of Cluny, told by an actual disciple of Odo, we are treated to a few homely, credible details about the man— his diet, his education, his daily conduct—and we are told also that the biographer, John of Salerno (an Italian contemporary of Aelfric's), was suspicious of those who liked to "praise exorcists, raisers of the dead, and all the other people famous for miracles." Yet the biographer himself reported many miraculous events, such as breadcrumbs turning to pearls, and a wild boar entering a poor church and willingly giving itself up to the assembly to be slaughtered. Also, he thought it necessary to apologize for digressions from the saintly formula, which he described explicitly as a movement from "the beginning of a holy life . . . fraught with difficulties and labors," to the end, which "brings glory and praise." This biography, filling a hundred pages, was fuller and more credible than any of Aelfric's "lives," and probably was so because it came from a more urban culture.

Saint Odo, who lived in feudal France, was not confronted by fiendish emperors. Unlike the early martyrs, he was not an alien spirit in his country, and he turned biographer on his own, doing the life of a saint some years his senior, Saint Gerald. Gerald also could do no wrong, and also performed many miracles, but unlike Odo, he was thoroughly secular, a feudal lord. Odo, though full of apologies for this anomaly, presented Gerald as a real, though model, person, by actually describing him physically. He was "of medium height and well-proportioned" with a "shining white" neck. He was also a count with a great demesne and hundreds of serfs under his rule, as well as great responsibilities for fighting off enemy lords. He grew up to his inheritance and his virtue, never married, lived temperately and piously but also vigorously, defeating enemies without hurting them, fending off robbers without punishing them, liberating his serfs (sometimes) but living within his own feudal-noble fate. Odo had to struggle to fit him to sainthood, but succeeded. Both he and Saint Gerald were—and I think still are—exceptions in the world of hagiography, which has remained remarkably resistant to change. St. Odo of Cluny, by John of Salerno, also contains the life of Saint Gerald (see Primary Readings).

The biographer must be a discoverer, not merely an embellisher. He cannot enter upon his enterprise in moral earnestness if the main ingredients of the enterprise are not his to examine critically, meditate upon, control. Ah, but hagiography still lives. Let me then stop complaining and point to what may be the most attractive feature of Aelfric's *Lives*. They were well made.

They were put together like short stories—the conventional, old-fashioned kind—with the intent of making a single splash. Aelfric always had the principle of omission working steadily in them to produce a clean narrative line: a beginning, middle, and end; a solid plot with suspense, climax, denouement, all the trappings; and, holding it together, an unambiguous, hammered-at moral. Granted, a short-story writer not into hagiography might wish to cut down on Aelfric's load of editorial comment, yet even with his pulpit matter Aelfric was artful, having the hero or heroine speak the homilies rather than intruding upon the tale himself. He was an excellent storyteller, and if he had lived in our time, he would have had trouble escaping the devil's enticements into soaps. Religious soaps.

Think of the scene in "The Life of St. Eugenia, Virgin," when Eugenia, accompanied by her two eunuch companions, and for infinite reasons dressed as a male, was accused by a wicked, conniving female, in front of her own Roman-judge father, of having attempted the seduction of said female. What did Eugenia do? Right, "she revealed her breast to the angry Philip / and said unto him, 'thou are my father!' " And Philip the father was properly amazed, and was immediately converted to Christ.

There are virtues here, and if they are not the virtues of truth makers, they still have a bearing upon biography. The genre does need more than truth makers, and its ancient practitioners sometimes knew this. Aelfric certainly did. Particularly for his early Christian purpose the genre needed life material, even though suspect, *not* in the lives of emperors and generals but in lonely human figures without rank and status—both male and female—wandering over the earth between life and death. After Aelfric's time the churches would create their own worldly leaders, and the worldly leaders would continue to bulk large in both human affairs and biography, but at least with these early accounts, the mean and trivial folk of society were permitted to *enter* the genre. It was a breakthrough, a great one, though even now an uncertain one for biography, hidden behind the miracles and the melodrama.

And thematically Aelfric's artistry led him to forceful simplicities of statement that are not found in the likes of Plutarch, simplicities like those in much contemporary popular film and TV drama. He melodramatically gave his saints wills of iron. They were Christian soldiers all, marching as to war, and their wars were on earth, and successful too. They were successful because the martyrs had power, earthly power. Did it matter that the power was from the Lord? Practically, not a bit. In our time, Aelfric's saints can be compared quite specifically and in detail to Marie of the movie *Marie* (see the Introduction) and even to our Batman-Superman species. Thus, in trying to put down Saint George, the wicked emperor Datian hired a sorcerer and said to George, "*Overcome* his magic, or let him *overcome* thee." (Of course George did overcome the sorcerer, who then became a Christian convert). As for Saint Agnes, she "*contended* through faith with the fiendlike rulers"—and was victorious. And Saint Basil did "*defeat* the bloodthirsty Julian's purpose." And Saint Eugenia, doing her duty comprehensively, "by martyrdom *overcame* the world." All of Aelfric's martyrs were warrior-willed, and their leader in heaven—quick with earthquake, lightning, and pestilence— was too. I acknowledge that between these early martyrs and, say, Eliot's Becket there is indeed an increase of *awareness* of self, and of its depths, but I do not think that awareness—or the lack of it—is the only biographical issue historically, or even the main one. What most needs to be noted is plain self-centeredness or its absence, which is a different matter. With the arrival of Christianity the self, simple but willful, began to assert its centrality in Western thought. Hence neither the Renaissance nor the Age of Science was needed to bring its isolate, acultural character to the fore, since by those times that character had already established itself.

The biographical consequences of the Christian concentration upon self can be clearly seen by calling to mind Plutarch's account of the last days of his favorite, Lycurgus, and noting how insistent Plutarch was that the dying Lycurgus sought out that which he had always preached in life, the diminution of self-will. Having (by dubious means) obtained a promise from his countrymen that they would obey the laws he had instituted until his return, he just headed for unknown parts and was never seen again. A neat political trick it was, but it meshed well with his ethic of self. He was not one to indulge the "higher vice," and as a result, Plutarch tells us, "the rule of life followed by one wise and temperate man" became the nation's rule for many generations, without the "unjust usurpations and despotisms" that had preceded him as a result of "avarice and luxury."

Of course Plutarch was prejudiced, and of course Lycurgus may be blamed for producing a nation of obedient military robots, but my point is that the Lycurgus fable seems at least to constitute a significantly different recipe for the making of suitable biographees. None of Aelfric's saints left town that way.

III

Three Italians: Machiavelli, Cellini, and Vasari

Now come three Renaissance figures. All were Italian, and all were molders of biography, though two did not think of themselves as biographers. First there is Niccolò Machiavelli, Shakespeare's predecessor in creating credible Renaissance leader-models. Second there is Benvenuto Cellini, his very own model, who enlivened the art of self-portraiture but also suggested a new direction for biography. And third there is Giorgio Vasari, a chronicler of art and artists, who nudged biography away from both kings and saints, and is my main target. All three of these writers helped give meaning to the phrase "Renaissance man," and the meaning they gave it was everywhere touched with resistance to old beliefs.

Machiavelli

Niccolò Machiavelli (1469–1527) is so familiar, so heavy on library shelves, that I must be referential and brief, lest I grind to a stop with him, and him alone. He moved in upon Western political thought, and upon the theater, with such force that his theories must have seemed a great novelty at the time, though it is not always clear what his theories were taken to be. Ostensibly he was an historian; that is, he derived his political theory from the study of history, starting with Livy's *History of Rome* and moving forward to his own extensive and disillusioning experience as a civil functionary in Florence and as a Florentine emissary to surrounding states. Yet, for him, theorizing really took precedence over cases. As a scholar he focused on abstract man, political man, man as a leader. And with a strange mixtureof cynicism and idealism about abstract man, he arrived, somehow, at his celebratedly radical postulates about leadership.

Leadership, not leaders. For at root he was not much interested in people. His most important work, *The Prince*, was not of the order of a chronicle or a life, but rather a set of curious principles for public conduct. He seems to have taken the murderer Cesare Borgia as a model for his "prince," but he also, at another time, took the same man to be one "devoid of pity . . . rebelling against Christ . . . a hydra . . . a basilisk." The contradiction has been explained in various ways,* but it certainly suggests a lack of interest in character per se.

Before writing *The Prince*, Machiavelli was for fourteen years an administrator and diplomat in Florence. Having been born to middle-class parents—his father a lawyer, his mother a "very cultured woman" writing "hymns to the virgin"—he was literate and serviceable, and also mindful of the power and money around him. He became an expert on the diplomatic relations between Florence and surrounding states, and on armies—their composition, strengths, and weaknesses. He traveled on sensitive diplomatic missions, especially to France and the Vatican, earning the confidence of some, and the distrust of others, as he gained knowledge of the *craft* of power. He married, was moderately unfaithful, and did not treat women as intellectual equals unless they were in positions of power. Seeking the unification of Italy, he became a thoroughgoing nationalist, and for his enthusiasm was pushed into retirement.

From retirement he was pushed into jail, then released and pushed into retirement again. By the time of his second retirement he was at work on his ambitious historical opus, *The Discourses*, but he put it aside to produce *The Prince*—really a condensed version of *The Discourses*—in the hope of getting his job back. He did not. He dedicated *The Prince* to Lorenzo (II) the Magnificent, of the Medici family, to whom he had been opposed but now was driven (by the threat of

---

* Machiavelli's biographer Jeffrey Pulver has done so by saying, "Machiavelli saw two Borgias, one, the leader in action, the man who by strength of will, his determination, his restless activity and his desire to put down anarchy and rule the conquered state with justice, and the other, the man Cesare with all his inherited vices." But where is there *consideration* of the vices?

foreign occupation of Florence) to favor. And in the last chapter he spoke directly to Lorenzo, bemoaning the fragmentation of Italy—"beaten, despoiled and overrun"—and looking to Lorenzo as its savior. He talked of the "illustrious house" of the Medici, and saw in its "exalted . . . power and fortune" hope that within it now there was someone who would heal Italy's wounds. But his heavy Machiavellian praise did not work with Lorenzo II.*

In fact Machiavelli comes down to us as unsuccessful at his own trade, and aware that he was. In a letter to a friend, written while he was finishing The Prince in "exile" on his own farm outside Florence, he said: "My poverty is a guarantee of my fidelity and honesty." He was never able to serve a prince again, and barely died in time to be spared the misery of watching even his minimal hope, Lorenzo II, removed by a foreigner.

Nevertheless, with us he is one of the famous idea men behind the modern state. He has even been called the founder of political science, though a better word might be art. In a forceful preface to the Modern Library edition of The Prince and The Discourses, Max Lerner summed him up as "the man who above all others taught the world to think in terms of cold political power." Lerner's praise—for it was meant as that—is just.

But I can not personally be as pleased with the man as Lerner was. Also, without defending him I want to combat Lerner's suggestion that power was his whole game. To think so is to neglect the side of Machiavelli that is relevant to this essay: his obsession, narrow but steady, with virtue.

I cannot deny that wherever the word virtue appeared in his work there was apt to be irony. Take, for instance, the introduction to The Discourses, where he put forth his plan for proceeding through Livy's History, commented on the rage for the virtues of antiquity that he found around him in his own culture, and then said that the virtues were "more admired than imitated." He proposed "to draw mankind from this error" by having it resume imitation of "the examples of antiquity," but he then quickly demonstrated that all the best examples of antiquity were, after all, only seeming-virtuous. In fact these

---

* Machiavelli may have at least enjoyed the irony of dedicating The Prince to Lorenzo the Magnificent without including the "II." Lorenzo I had been the magnificent one, a strong and good Medici, and influential in Machiavelli's own childhood upbringing.

antique models practiced deceit like excellent Machiavellians. For all this apparent contempt for the virtuous, I find earnestness in him on the worn subject.

I mean earnestness about real virtue, though now I may have to write a book about the "real," which I thought to do when I was young and strong. Machiavelli vacillated between irony and indignation at the absence of virtue around him, and I find that mixture indicative of deep feeling. In one paragraph he would refuse to "censure anyone for having employed any extraordinary means for the purpose of establishing a kingdom or constituting a republic," and in another he would belabor the morality of those means as if the means *mattered*, mattered the way they would have mattered to Plutarch. Of a Sicilian tyrant, for instance, he said, surely angrily: "It cannot be called virtue to kill one's fellow citizens, betray one's friends, be without faith, without pity, and without religion; by these means one may indeed gain power, but not glory."

The easy explanation for these switches is that Renaissance Italian culture simply would not let Machiavelli leave the subject of virtue alone. That culture made capital of virtue, could not get along without it. Even with the Borgias in the Vatican, he had to build his theories around virtue's sticky, hypocritical presence.

But a more interesting explanation is that he was, though disillusioned, still basically respectful of virtue, in the way that the noble Greeks and Romans had been, and that he was promoting respect for conscientious leaders who exercised their best energies to produce an orderly society.

We probably know the cynical side of Machiavelli best. For instance, we know how often he targeted the seemingly religious, pushing the paradox that a prince, especially a new prince, is often obliged "to act against faith, against charity, against humanity, and against religion," even while taking "great care" to "seem to be all mercy, faith, integrity, humanity and religion." A less familiar but equally sour side of him appeared in an excellent farce he wrote while in "exile" on his farm. Its title was *Mandragola*. It had in it both a seeming-virtuous friar, who became a model of money-grubbing hypocrisy, and a truly virtuous wife, who happily became *un*virtuous. The plot progressed through elaborate actions that were designed to make villainy, not virtue, triumphant. In the end the cuckold of the play was persuaded by a whole team of Machiavellians to let the lover of his pure wife go to bed with her. In fact he was persuaded to *put* the lover into the bed with her and to "feel how things were going." The editor and translator of a recent edition in English, Henry Paolucci, notes that the "ultimate object of the plot . . . [was] to effect in the wife a fundamental transvaluation of values."

On the earnest side Machiavelli went after the Roman Church hard on simple moral grounds. It was decadent. It did not follow the principles upon which Christianity had been founded. Not only was it rotten within, but its "evil example" had "destroyed all piety and religion in Italy." Like a true admirer of ancient virtues, he thus declared his preference for primitive over present religious practices.

And this preference extended to the ancient non-Christians too. Like an old Roman, he was not at all cynical about the virtue that was "manly spirit; bravery; valor; daring; courage; physical and intellectual excellence." In fact he was especially strong on intellectual excellence. Plutarch would have liked him for that, but would have liked him better if intellectual excellence had not so often taken the form, with him, of great cleverness, a great capacity to strategize. Plutarch's focus had been on rationality and foresight. Machiavelli imposed the meaning "craft" upon the word *virtue*, which led perhaps to the current meaning in English for *virtù*—roughly, "native artfulness." But he did so without abandoning older meanings. He was a thoroughly grave person about public service. Combining deceit with statesmanship was therefore a grave, not a cynical, undertaking for him.

Naturally, young idealists have trouble with him here. They think that deceit and virtue are incompatible, and that combining them is a form of doublethink, until they have been properly indoctrinated in realpolitik, perhaps through a college course in political science. In such a course they are told that deceit is a necessary and respectable part of the public-service trade (except, perhaps, when practiced by the enemy), and they become grave persons too. Machiavelli did much to bring credibility to this moral anomaly, a credibility that is not, I think, evident in Plutarch.

Yet Machiavelli did no more than Plutarch with the private life of virtue. If anything, he was blinder than Plutarch to the private thoughts and feelings of public men. The character of his model prince is as limited as the types in his farce, *Mandragola*. In the farce it does not matter. The cuckold, the doting lover, the virtuous wife who suffers instant transvaluation, and all the crafty manipulators are placed in a complex plot involving so much mistaken identity that true identity is not a factor. But true identity does matter for the prince. What sort of model for the grave spirits of the world is he? We never learn. He is a bundle of crafty reflexes rather than a possible person. He is not allowed to pause in his machinations, to take a siesta from public affairs. He lives right down the hall from Marcus Aurelius, though readers like Max Lerner do not think so. Marcus Aurelius is upright, Machiavelli's prince seems upright—but within the limited frame of public morality the difference does not really matter.

In *Othello* Iago says to his dupe, Roderigo, who has provoked him by declaring that it is not in his "virtue" to pull off a betrayal, "Virtue! A fig! 'Tis in ourselves that we are thus and thus," thereby telling the dupe something Machiavellian that Machiavelli would not have said. By way of explanation Iago added: "Our bodies are our gardens, to which our wills are gardeners." Iago, courtesy of Shakespeare, was as much obsessed with virtue as Machiavelli, but what he did that Machiavelli did not do was posit the self as a positive individual force, something to be reckoned with on its own. (Thus Iago, a loner, was certainly to be reckoned with *as* a loner in the play.) Machiavelli's prince was oddly lacking in that kind of selfness (or selfishness), lacking in precisely the quality that made Machiavellianism such a fine philosophy for villains like Iago. Machiavelli's prince had a blank inside him where the selfish quality should have been (how can one be a true villain without private motives?), so that he could act virtuously or villainously in achieving his ends, yet remain virtuous, because the ends—the public ends—were always virtuous. He was a public servant, serving his country.

In the modern world of biography there is now a whole subgenre in which that assumption lurks. The assumption goes back to Aristotle, though deviously. It makes the private life trivial, hence puts it out of play. So each year dozens of political biographies appear in which we learn what it was that Roosevelt said in memos to his advisers before he ran for a third term, what Kennedy's expressed doubts about the Bay of Pigs were a few days in advance of the invasion, who angered Johnson in the Rose Garden during the dark days of Vietnam, and so on. We learn so much, in fact, that if we did our homework properly, we would have no room left in our heads for anything else. For whole libraries full of such information are constantly plumbed by scholars, and an enormous amount of documentation of a certain kind is taken to be private, in the sense of unofficial and previously undisclosed. Unfortunately it is private only in the Machiavellian sense in which deceit-as-policy is private. For our immense political biographies are preponderantly studies of the strategies of public figures in historic moments. They are light-years away from the tales of just one "soul . . . moving between two definite events, birth and death."

How odd it is that Machiavelli, the great denigrator of virtuous conduct among the great, was one of the key figures to pass on the Plutarchian tradition of biography. Yet that was his role. If we look for the influence of Plutarch in modern biography, we find it in institutes of realpolitik, disguised as Machiavellian strategizing. Here is a passage from *The Discourses* that sounds to me depressingly like a good many modern history texts with an orientation to statecraft:

> When . . . Francis, Duke of Angouleme, succeeded to the throne of France, he desired to recover for his kingdom the Duchy of Milan, which a few years previously had been taken by the Swiss, with the aid of Pope Julius II. For this purpose he wanted to have allies in Italy to facilitate his enterprise; and besides the Venetians, whom King Louis had already gained over, he tried to secure the support of the Florentines and of Pope Leo X, deeming their alliance most important to his success, inasmuch as the king of Spain had troops in Lombardy, and the forces of the Emperor of Germany held Verona. The Pope, however, did not yield to the solicitations of the French king, but was persuaded by his counsellors (according to report) to remain neutral.

I had not meant to quote so much, but the passage has a fascinating consistency. Here is an assortment of great leaders desiring, wanting, deeming, soliciting, and being persuaded to gain allies, facilitate a military enterprise, and recover a kingdom—or remain neutral. So the king of France wants the duchy of Milan, and within the circle of his desire the Swiss, the Vatican, the Venetians, the Florentines, the king of Spain, and the emperor of Germany circulate. Passing a test in class on Francis's problem would not be easy, yet the *desire* of Francis—which started the whole business—is just there, a given: King Francis "desired to recover for his kingdom the Duchy of Milan"! This kind of history is loosely tied to classical biography by virtue of being a history of a few willful leaders asserting their wills. This kind of history is still with us today, and it still tends to confirm Burckhardt's observations about the lack of awareness of self among the *ancients*—though I would call this lack of awareness more nearly an ignoring of self. That this kind of history should be Machiavelli's contribution to the Renaissance is ironic, since Burckhardt pointed to the Renaissance as the age of the discovery of self. The best one can do is not blame Machiavelli for that discovery. He was an historian and had been studying the Greeks and Romans.

The above passage is, however, more detailed than Machiavelli usually was, and comes closer to historical facts. Machiavelli was not as respectful of facts as Plutarch. He used history with haste and did not scruple to draw large conclusions with equal haste. His conclusions had the sound of Plutarch but not the solidity. Here is an example from *The Discourses*, a balanced abstracting of the good and the bad, which is supposed to be applicable to any historical situation:

> And as the reformation of the political condition of a state presupposes a good man, whilst the making of himself prince of a republic by violence naturally presupposes a bad one, it will consequently be extremely rare that a good man should be found willing to employ wicked means to become prince, even though his final object be good; or that a bad man, after having become prince, should be willing to labor for good ends, and that it should enter his mind to use for good purposes that authority which he has acquired by evil means.

The presuppositions here, and the assumptions about the motivations of hypothetical princes, are—despite Max Lerner—thoroughly unmodern. In their sweep they sound a little like Aristotle's prescriptions for a tragic hero, who could not be bad but could not be wholly good either. As an historian Plutarch would not have wished—though the *mode* of judgment seems to be loosely his—to isolate judgment so completely from an historical context. Nor, I think, would he have approved such an arbitrary separation of the black hats from the white hats. Plutarch may not have plumbed the private depths of human character, but he did not make easy assumptions about it either. Machiavelli, despite his great influence upon the history of public virtue, seems to have had a moral attitude rather like that of a movie director toward westerns.

Benvenuto Cellini

And now, with Benvenuto Cellini, a bit more about autobiography. Its grandeurs and delusions. The only comprehensive book on its beginnings that I am familiar with is one I have already referred to, Georg Misch's excellent *History of Autobiography in Antiquity*, the first edition of which goes back to 1907. In it Misch worried at length about where autobiography began, noting the many deceptive instances of first-person usage in ancient times, such as old Indian "birth stories," which tell, in the first person, of some five hundred fifty births of Buddha, births such as this one: "And again in another life I was a young hare, living in a mountain forest; I ate grass and herbs, leaves and fruits, and did evil to no being" (ca. 480 B.C.).

Misch discovered instructive mixtures of real life with fable in earlier Egyptian narratives, but settled, as I must, on putting such matter outside the realm of autobiography. Somehow storytelling was separate—even at the beginning of significant generic difference—from accounts of personal lives, and the effect of the separation was probably healthy, putting autobiography ahead of biography itself in the plumbing of human character.

As I have said, biography picked up much of its early energy from the telling of fables—in the form of narrative and dramatic poetry, and particularly in the "model" tradition of tragedy. In biography, as in tragedy, the chosen subjects were exceptional people whose *actions* made them exceptional. Autobiography had leeway for the life of the self: what the subjects thought, how they came in their own minds to their actions, and what the actions meant to them.

Misch pointed to an autobiographical passage in Plato's *Republic* as an early move toward "self-realization," an account of Plato's youthful experiences with politicians who were grounded not in philosophy but in hard knocks. Plato found the confusion in the politicos' affairs so great that it bothered him physically, making him first indignant and finally "dizzy" as he groped for remedies. The passage is convincingly real as a description of private feeling, but as Misch said, it was a rarity. Also, in context it was merely incidental to making Plato's favorite impersonal point about the need for philosopher-kings.

Another instance mentioned by Misch was more clearly a true forerunner of autobiography. In it the rhetorician Isocrates tried to give a report, of sorts, of his whole life, and also entered upon the task "for its own sake" (thereby meeting Misch's criterion of exclusion of persons like Plato who wished to use private events only illustratively and in passing). Isocrates' "life" had a flaw, though, one the genre has not yet mended (certainly Cellini did not). It was encomiastic rather than investigative. It was a long labor of self-glorification.

Misch then singled out the memoirs of various Roman emperors, and especially those of the first emperor, Augustus (63 B.C.– A.D. 14) as the most impressive classical efforts at autobiography. They could not have been produced, Misch felt, "if the point of view represented had not lived in the consciousness of the author as utter reality"— that is, as Augustus's own. And though they were loaded with self-praise and self-justification, they were also filled with detailed off-hand remarks about private, unstrategic love affairs. Saint Augustine, a bit later, would have agonized about that, for in reporting on a private life there was no need to display uprightness. The public life was the home of the moral life.

Here, surely, was a beginning of the separation of autobiography from grave and pure models. Unfortunately the emperors had large egos but little expressed inclination to inspect them. Yet Augustine, whose fifth-century *Confessions* are sometimes referred to as the first autobiography, had no great inclination either. His ego inspections were of a kind that produced only unlocalized conclusions. We have to move to the Renaissance—with Burckhardt but without Machiavelli—to find substantial *reachings* for self-knowledge. And in my opinion we do not find a great deal even there.

Not at least in Benvenuto Cellini. What began with Cellini was not a demonstration of self-knowledge so much as a sudden, full-blown individualism. As the crossword puzzlers say, he was a "oner." (I have never run across this word except in puzzles, but it is a word, and I now give it to biography.) He had an ego as big as any emperor's, but unlike the emperors, he had no reason to think of himself as a collective "I." He was just Benvenuto Cellini, of the Florentine Cellinis, and right at the beginning of his autobiography he showed that he knew perfectly well the high rank of those who *usually* wrote in the genre. Mockingly he described his "humble birth," then said of it that in fact it was most illustrious. Why? Because it was a Florentine birth and Florence was illustrious. The first democrat? No, for then he settled in to demonstrate to the world, without mockery, that he himself was illustrious.

So far as I can see, Cellini did this without any knowledge of the classical tradition of the encomium. He was no rhetorician. His tale of himself was not an argument, not an organized "proof" of his great felicities. In some ways it was a fine early example of an episodic, picaresque novel—and might well have been called "The Adventures of Benvenuto"—but it was not intended as such. It was intended as autobiography, and in it Cellini was at all times impossibly egocentric, his own hero, so taken by the role that he did not need to step out of it to ask himself if what he was reporting was of public import. It had to be of public import if Benvenuto lived it. Later autobiographers might solace themselves with thoughts of the spiritual rewards to be had in recording merely private matters, but not he. Even in private he thought of himself as a fine public model for all.

As a braggart he was at least light-hearted, with a sharp, satiric tongue, and this clearly separates him from the high tradition of Aristotle's grave spirits. Cellini's heroic pretensions were always present, but so, pleasantly, was the spirit of the mean, the socially-morally-spiritually trivial. And the mean, as Aristotle stuffily pointed out, was the spirit for comedy. Cellini's life was a mix of the heroic and comic—a charming and influential mix.

By the age of fifteen Benvenuto was a master goldsmith, a fearless fighter with any weapon, and a saintly, supportive son to his old father. At sixteen he was grown, well traveled, and a man among women. At nineteen he was in Rome amazing the goldsmiths there, battling dozens of enemies at once (as with sophisticated western movies it is sometimes hard to *tell* the white hats from the black hats), being discovered by the rich and famous, becoming a truly great lover, and having pleasant chats with Pope Clement.

Then the good Pope Clement died and was replaced by the wicked Pope Paul, who imprisoned Benvenuto and had him sentenced to death, but then had a drinking bout with a cardinal pleading for Benvenuto's life during which, before vomiting, the pope said to the cardinal: "This very instant I want you to take him home with you."

It was also about this time that Cellini was able to help a surgeon save a beautiful girl's life. He did so by making, in five minutes, "a very delicate little steel tool, curved, and sharp enough for a razor." The girl's father came to love him "as much or even more than he loved his two sons."

And so, for four hundred pages, it went for Benvenuto, as he made friends and enemies but astonished both with his strength, courage, precocity, and artistic genius. Here was material for a novel for sure, or at least Renaissance oater material (I think at least one movie has been made of Cellini's life—with Errol Flynn? Douglas Fairbanks, Jr.?), but not material that Aristotle's grave spirits would have found grave. It was too extravagant, too much of the order of tall-tale telling, too undisciplined, loose, free-and-easy. Aristotle's grave spirits were nothing if not disciplined, and their disciplined thoughts about self-conduct dominated the art they practiced. A tragedy was flawed if it did not conform to Aristotle's rules for its structure. And biographies such as Plutarch's also were flawed if they were not neat and trim.

As for the hagiographers, they had changed the direction a self was to move in to be grave—from Athens to heaven—but they had disapproved of self-indulgence as much as the grave pagans. Even when the saints spoke of themselves, as Augustine did, it was always to deny the self liberties, to insist on purity, purity, purity. As a result the saints' lives, as written, were neat and trim too—no digressions permitted on the road to heaven.

Benvenuto was not a grave spirit like any of these, and his self-indulgence in life was matched by his indulgence as a writer. He was not one to pass on balanced assessments of himself, to compose neat homilies, or to round out a narrative according to some critic's specifications. He just rambled—and sometimes raved, and sometimes joked—and so managed to please thousands of readers in later ages who have come to think of purity and discipline as both dull and deceiving properties of the self. Selves' lives *are*, after all, loose and rambling.

But because Benvenuto was deeply in love with himself he could not be *merely* low and comfortable with his adventures, as Cervantes' Sancho was. His delusions of grandeur were too grand. At the time of his imprisonment by wicked Pope Paul he had a number of visions comparable to those reported by the Christian saints. He found himself miraculously visited by God Himself, who with the Madonna in attendance emerged right out of the sun, with angels, twice. In other words he was often more like Don Quixote himself than Sancho, and as serious about becoming a great goldsmith as a knight could be about serving the lovely Dulcinea del Toboso.

Yet as an artist he at least had the *right*, the moral right, to be just Sancho, one of the mean. For simply by being what he was he was a nonleader, someone who was not expected to have only public thoughts in print. He was not a commissioner but one commissioned, not patron but patronee.

The difference showed on every page of his book. He was honored, yes, and well paid, for the Renaissance was the greatest of art ages. But being honored as an artist did not mean that he was obliged to be a model human. Only his work was caught in the model trap, an important displacement that left his to-be-written-about self free to do what Benvenuto's self did in fact do: eat, drink, and try to be whole.

It was in his complicated relations with his many patrons that his new freedoms were most apparent. True, what he reported was always exaggerated. He would say that the king of France never went out without being trailed by twelve thousand horsemen, and then, pleased with the number, repeat it for emphasis, saying, "In peacetime, when the court is complete, there are eighteen thousand, and so with twelve thousand the number is at the lowest." But even at a discount his tales show a respect, a devotion to the rights and privileges of genius that was not wind. The great patrons around him believed him because he believed himself.

And with his great faith and enthusiasm he usually had the patrons where he wanted them. The patrons had a Veblenian lust for appearances (see some of Browning's Renaissance poems), and the artists had been put into the world to provide them with these. A cardinal would compete with a king, a duke with a pope, for an elegant bowl or (Cellini's greatest work) a saltcellar. In many of the great patrons the lust was even refined, so that they knew, aesthetically, what it was they lusted after: beauty, grace, elegance. When they commissioned a work they were not just ordering something to put on a table or fill a wall with (or gain high investment returns from); they were showing their good taste, culture, refinement. So when they tried to prescribe to the artist what it was they wanted, the artist had them where he wanted them—if only he could be self-assertive.

Cellini's most successful pushy moment was perhaps the time he berated the not-very-good cardinal who had rescued him from the wicked Pope Paul. The cardinal was lusting after the still-unfinished saltcellar, and trying to specify how it should be wrought. But Cellini, with several other great patrons in attendance, told him "how important the sons of kings and emperors" were, yet how quickly "a poor humble shepherd" would prefer his own sons to these. Then he switched, poor humble shepherd that he was not, to his preference for his "own work and invention" over something created by others. He emerged, of course, the winner, and proceeded to do the saltcellar just as he had wanted to.

And the results were uniformly stupendous. Of an even lesser work than the saltcellar the king of France himself said (Benvenuto had no problem with direct quotations): "I am certain such beautiful work was never known to ancients. I remember well having seen all the best works done by the finest craftsmen of Italy, but I never saw any that moved me more than this." The king in question was Francis I, whom Benvenuto described as an enlightened idiot. This king managed to get the saltcellar away from the cardinal, and paid Benvenuto well, giving him "a servant on horseback to look after [his] needs," granting him unlimited freedom over his own life and conduct, and praising him incessantly. He was so pleased with Benvenuto's small, elegant pieces that one day Benvenuto sat him down and proposed to make him something a bit bigger, comprising five figures, the one in the middle to be 54 feet high. "At this the King made a tremendous gesture of amazement." All five figures were to be richly symbolic too. "The king hardly had the patience to let me finish before he said in a loud voice, 'In very truth, I've found a man after mine own heart.' "

Somewhere in the middle of these extravagances Cellini did at least two fine things for autobiography—and for biography too, indirectly. First, he freed the writer from the grip of spiritual gravity, letting him deal equably, for instance, with that beast the human body. Cellini loved the human body, male or female, in or out of bed, in public squares or atop saltcellars—and virtue entered not at all into his thoughts of it, except aesthetically. Second, he gave the genre more of a sense of the *presence* of self on a page than perhaps anyone before him. Not that he was introspective—he was too arrogant and outgoing to be that—but he was somehow able, in the words of Georg Misch, to "show the spirit brooding over the recollected material." That spirit was immanent in his work, whether he thought he was brooding or not, and I agree with Misch that that spirit, for which another word may be *style*, is probably "the most important real element in autobiography."

It is in dealing with that spirit, though, that biographers are handicapped. They cannot themselves write in that other spirit wholly, though if they are good they can sometimes catch it. Also, they will sometimes find it simply dangerous even to try to write in that spirit, since they have a greater obligation to be objective than to commune. Yet at all times they can at least work to *describe* that spirit adequately, its special, individual qualities. Oddly, biographers up to the time of the Renaissance had not really thought of doing that.

Giorgio Vasari

Giorgio Vasari's *Lives of the Artists* is a true but limited classic, much alive today at art schools and colleges. In an abbreviated paperback version recently published by Penguin, the skill of the translator, George Bull (who has also translated Cellini for Penguin), is such that for better or worse Vasari now sounds, in English, like a contemporary art historian. With outdated views.

Then there is the massive, elegant, three-volume edition published by Abrams, complete with pictures and an introduction by Kenneth Clarke. Vasari is *in* now, a regular part of art history courses as they rage through the ages.

He is also a part of Victorian poetry courses as they rage through Robert Browning. Vasari was for Browning a little like what Holinshed was for Shakespeare, and it is always pleasing to see what poets steal from their helpless ancestors. Browning not only wrote his "Fra Lippo Lippi" and "Andrea del Sarto" with Vasari at his elbow (he had Dante there too), but he also took a bit of Vasari's whole view of things, and something of Vasari's tone and manner. Vasari was bumptious, expansive, optimistic, opinionated, and, like Browning's characters, never at a loss for words. He knew what he knew.

Like Cellini he was a Renaissance man. Cellini despised him, but they had much in common. Both were artists, and both were convinced that their age had at last arrived at the heights of human endeavor, thanks to artists. They were surrounded by artists, in a culture that had patrons for artists, and time for artists, and respect for artists. Vasari seemed to think there was little going for humanity in the sixteenth century *except* art and artists.

Naturally, much was being written by and about artists at the time, yet no one seems to have tried to do what Vasari set out to do, either in his culture or before him. He took his cue from the chroniclers, whose loose format he loosely followed, and simply shifted his focus from princes and saints (and their accomplishments) to art heroes (and their art).

Cellini despised him because he had done Cellini a "bad turn" with a certain duke. Cellini called him "little Giorgio Vasari" and "an envious enemy." He complained that Vasari had gone to bed with one Manno, a "good-natured young man" whom Cellini thought of as his own, and "had taken the skin off one of Manno's legs, with those filthy little claws whose nails he never cut." But as George Bull notes, Cellini was "a monster of prejudice."

Vasari must have known what Cellini wrote of him, for in his own brief biography of Cellini he excused its brevity by saying that Cellini had "written of his own life and works with much more eloquence and order than I perchance would be able to use here"; but with his eye on art rather than artist he praised the man reservedly, saying that he surpassed the ancients in the making of medals (just the sort of thing Cellini said of himself), was "the most famous goldsmith of his day, and a distinguished sculptor." Vasari was too smart to be a monster, being an encomiast in principle and practice.

Like Cellini, he was of "humble birth," but he did not brag about it. He talked little of himself directly, though he was personal in his judgments and did not hesitate to use the first person or to slip in a plug for his role in dozens of art projects. His was a tradesman's family with artist connections. They had little money but a good eye for upward mobility. When Giorgio, at the age of nine, was found busy reading and scribbling pictures, they put him with an artist to be trained, and saw to it that he was quickly discovered by an emissary of the pope who happened to be passing through. The emissary was a cardinal, no less, and soon Giorgio was sent to Rome to study with Michaelangelo, who was too busy and sent him to Andrea del Sarto. Vasari also quickly picked up a patron, the duke with whom Cellini said Vasari had damaged him, and he benefited from the duke's largess until the duke was murdered. Then for some years he was a busy transient, moving from commission to commision around Italy and becoming well known as a painter at the same time that he felt the pulse of the art world around him and developed his idea for his book. A busy bee, he had the first edition of the book published when he was still in his thirties. By then his humble beginning was behind him. He was well known, propertied, and close to the mighty. His happy condition showed on every page of his book.

A busy bee. By the time of the second edition, he had done something like one hundred sixty "lives" in all. Some were only a few pages long (Cellini's was among the shortest: three pages), but most covered twenty to fifty pages. The longest (120 pages in the final version) was the life of Michaelangelo, whom Vasari worshiped. From the plain bulk of the tome we can see how disciplined and prolific he was at his trade. And from the many success messages scattered through the tome we can see how important he thought being disciplined and prolific was. Over and over the messages were the same: greatness in art came from being, aside from a genius, good at making connections, keeping an eye out for the main chance.

Thus, he wrote in one of the earliest "lives," Cimabue, a boy in Florence, kept busy scribbling his books with pictures and impressing certain nearby craftsmen who were decorating a chapel. Then he impressed the father superior of the chapel. Then he impressed King Charles of Anjou, who happened to be passing through Florence and joined with the men and women of the city in "jostling each other and rejoicing" about him.

Thus Giotto, a poor country boy who "was always sketching what he saw in nature," was seen scraping a design on a rock by none other than Cimabue and came, almost instantly, to be "recognized and honored for his genius" by the pope.

And thus Fra Lippo Lippi, an orphan trapped in a convent "scrawling pictures on his own books and those of others," was captured and enslaved by Moors, who were so astonished by his painting that they released him and (somehow) brought him to the attention of an astonished King Alphonso of Naples.

Vasari's formula was a little like one familiar form of the "American dream," the success stories of Horatio Alger. Upon inspection their moral turned out to be less that hard work will automatically bring its rewards than that one was to "work, save, be a good boy, shun the fleshpots, and presently the mining stock will fall into your lap."* As a Renaissance Italian, Vasari did not worry a great deal about the fleshpots—except as they distracted geniuses from their duties—but otherwise he had a thoroughly businesslike view of the road to success. One of his big jobs as biographer, he said, was to describe "the fine strokes, the expedients, and the prudent courses of action" used "by successful men in forwarding their enterprises."

The result of this view was that he honored the enterprises of his biographees much more than their lives. His focus may have been quite natural and proper for an art historian, but he was so heavily committed to the enterprises that he should have thought twice about calling his essays "lives" (and patting himself on the back occasionally for the truths therein). The essays were more nearly little Beideckerian journeys through the churches and galleries of Italy.

* From Frederick Lewis Allen's much-anthologized essay, "Horatio Alger, Jr." (1938). Most teachers of freshman composition of my generation "used" it.

His standard format was an opening summary of a man's accomplishments (women, of course, did not, exist as artists in Renaissance Italy; they steadily appeared in such literature as Cellini's and Vasari's as harlots, unfaithful wives, or conniving duchesses—despite the beauty that made them models), followed by a very brief description of his background and upbringing. Sometimes the upbringing was marked only by being discovered, but at any rate it preceded a long, fulsome accounting of the subject's individual works, then a quick account of his death, a recap, and praise for his talent. Vasari was perfunctory about the life, but tediously observant about the works, and could dash off paragraph after paragraph about a painting, cramming them with data like this:

> Below the choir in Santa Maria [Masaccio] painted a fresco showing the Trinity, which is over the alter of St. Ignatius and which has Our Lady on one side and St. John the Evangelist on the other, contemplating the crucified Christ. At the sides are two kneeling figures, which as far as one can tell are portraits of those who commissioned the work, although they can scarcely be made out as they have been covered over with ornamentation. But the most beautiful thing, apart from the figures, is the barrel-vaulted ceiling drawn in perspective and divided into square compartments containing rosettes foreshortened and made to recede so skillfully that the surface looks as if it is indented.

After a few thousand words about foreshortened rosettes the reader begins to feel a touristy longing for a quiet table in a sidewalk café; and if he has not at his elbow an expensive, complete collection of the works of the artist in question (who in every instance roamed the length and breadth of Italy, with forays into France, leaving his artmarks), he is lost.

In Vasari's time there must have been a profitably large prospective audience of tourists for such material, or he would not have been so lavish with it. He was a thoroughgoing art entrepreneur, a sort of Bruce Barton or Dale Carnegie of that business, so his "lives" verged on being practical lessons in profitable genius-conduct.

True, he had for models some of the most successful artists in history, but he also made good use of them. What he passed on is still useful source material for scholars, once they manage to filter out a few thousand foreshortened rosettes. True also, he had odd things to say about the artists he thought were *not* at the top, *not* in the mainstream, black sheep. But these views are useful too, revealing the limits of his aesthetic.

In his opinion Uccello, for instance, was a black sheep, being weak in art's "chief province, the reproduction of the human form." Uccello "found pleasure only in exploring certain difficult, or rather impossible, problems of perspective." Artists like Uccello examined things "too minutely" and were apt to "end up solitary, eccentric, melancholy and poor, as indeed did Paolo Uccello himself." The mainstream ran from Cimabue to Michelangelo, and paid well.

Vasari had a perfect mainstream mind at a perfect time. He knew what humanity had always wanted from art, and he traced its course down through the ages with the easy assurance of someone who is certain he is right. In his several prefaces he began, like the chroniclers, at the very beginning of (art) things, and then moved knowledgeably forward—he was a sophisticated generalist—to his own climactic time, thus molding the past to the standards of that time. Modern art historians may or may not think that art has been going downhill since Vasari, and may complain mildly or loudly of his rejecting Uccello, possibly even defending certain "Byzantine absurdities" he chose to damn; but to his praise for the great artists around him they can hardly take exception until he is done, at which time, after each life, the question is sure to arise. What did Vasari *look* for in his geniuses, beyond accuracy of reproduction and marvelously foreshortened rosettes? No one knew more than he of the shop-talk aspects of his culture's painting, sculpture, and architecture, but as a thinker beyond his own frame, he was limited. As Cellini said, he was "little Giorgio," and as "little Giorgio" he was a forerunner of much critical biography to come, in which the crucial relationship between a life and the art it produces—crucial, surely, if criticism and biography are to be successfully blended—is somehow supplanted by rosettes.

Aesthetically, Vasari's thinking hinged wholly on the human body, accurately represented, as the artist's "chief province," just, he reported, as it had for God in the Garden of Eden; and that hinge hinged Vasari's biographical thinking too. In classical times, he wrote, the movement in art was toward the perfect imitating of God's work as reflected in the story of Pygmalion. In Christian times, following the "complete botch" the Caesars and then the barbarians made of beauty, the movement was upward again, toward an inspired (I will return to that word) realism, though Christianity was not always helpful, since the Christians "ruined or demolished all the marvelous statues . . . representing false pagan gods" and for a time "all sense of form and good style was lost." With Cimabue, Vasari's first realist hero, and then Giotto, artists again began to "open the door of truth." Giotto especially "brought to life the great art of painting as we know it today, introducing the techniques of drawing accurately from life, which had been neglected for more than two hundred years."

From then on it was aesthetically clear sailing, with the realists appearing as friendly (sometimes) rivals in many many competitions, "exerting all their energies and knowledge to surpass one another," and jealously hiding what they were doing, lest they should copy one another's ideas. Vasari loved the competition in the business, reported on it in detail, and rushed to judgment himself. He found Lorenzo Ghiberti properly acclaimed for the "finished perfection" of the figures in the bronze doors of the Merchants' Guild of Florence. He bemoaned the villainy of Luca Borgo for trying "to blot out his teacher's name [Piero della Francesca] and to usurp for himself the honor which belonged entirely to Piero." And he remarked of Leonardo da Vinci that he left others "far behind," since absolutely everything that he did came "from God rather than human art." Of judgments he was full, but they were all—except when aimed at the likes of Uccello—remarkably favorable.

The Leonardo life is a good instance of how the encomiast in Vasari could lead him to gloss over crucial biographical matter, and aesthetic matter too. He presented Leonardo as a nearly perfect human being from birth, his greatest fault being a certain excess of perfectionism, which made him slow in finishing his works. He was a genius, that's all. He received his powers directly from God, and the powers could be seen in his technical skill. His works were "utterly convincing" in their "wonderful realism," showing "how faithfully art can imitate nature." And because of their reproductive precision, Vasari wrote, "we have a deeper understanding of human anatomy and the anatomy of the horse." The Mona Lisa was probably his greatest realistic display, and in it the eyebrows "were completely natural, growing thickly in one place and lightly in another, the mouth appeared to be living flesh rather than paint, [and] on looking closely at the pit of her throat one could swear that the pulses were beating."

Yes, but entirely missing from the account was any suggestion that the fidelity produced a Mona Lisa smile that seemed other than merely contented. Vasari said that while painting her, Leonardo had "employed singers musicians or jesters to keep her full of merriment and so chase away the melancholy that painters usually give to portraits." He made no mention of anything other than "merriment" in her finished expression.

Nor could he bring himself to find troubled looks in other works by Leonardo, except when there was *supposed* to be trouble, as with a painting of Judas. He could not allow shadows to creep across such artistry, and would have found Freud's study of Leonardo absolutely wild—as in fact it is. Pater led Freud to the darkness in Mona Lisa's expression, using the word *sinister*. But in analyzing the darkness of the portrait, Freud leapt to Leonardo's character, which he found to be unstable from (of course) childhood, when Leonardo was over-nursed by his "unsatisfied" mother. Freud discovered that Leonardo's mother "took her little son in place of her husband, and by the too early maturing of his eroticism robbed him of a part of his masculinity." Hence the child grew to maturity with a disgust for the act of procreation, and avoided it by intent devotion to his art and to science. ("He investigated instead of loving.") As a result a shadow fell on his life, which is visible in the Great Smile itself. *Leonardo da Vinci and a Memory of His Childhood* is one of Freud's most elaborate and controversial accounts, and its improvisations upon a single sentence in Leonardo's notebooks are as extended and diversionary as anything in *Tristram Shandy*. *

Between the extremes of Vasari's blindness and Freud's obsessive perception sit both ancient and modern biography.

When Vasari came to his mentor Michelangelo he had enough biographical material at hand to go more thoroughly into the life than with any other artist. Yet, despite his relative intimacy, his account was a purification rite from the beginning. There he announced that the genius of Leonardo and all the other artists of the world was as nothing beside Michelangelo's:

> The benign ruler of heaven graciously looked down to earth, saw the worthlessness of what was being done, the intense but utterly fruitless studies, and the presumption of men who were farther from true

---

* Leonardo described a dream he had of a vulture. Freud made sexual significance of the vulture, but *vulture* it apparently was not in the original Italian—as some critics of Freud have been happy to point out. Critics do, however, reckon—as Vasari did not—with the mystery of the Great Smile.

art than night is to day, and resolved to save us from our errors. So he decided to send into the world an artist who . . .

In this manner he canceled out all his earlier compliments—of such oddities is the world of the tribute made—but at least he had thematic reason for doing so. His life of Michelangelo was the last in the first edition of his collection (1550), the climax of his historical progression to perfect realism. In it he was able to give final shape to his program for human forms in marble and on canvas, and to assert that representational perfection was the whole aim in art. "Only by copying the human form, and by selecting from what was beautiful the most beautiful," could that aim be achieved.

With Michelangelo, he was able to dwell at length on the technique in Michelangelo's greatest works—pages and pages about the Sistine Chapel, panel by panel—and to indulge in the kind of lush praise he enjoyed. Thus he said of a marble Pietà that "a formless block of stone" had been "reduced to a perfection that nature is scarcely able to create in the flesh." And with Michelangelo's statue of David, he was able to climb even further aloft:

> The legs are skillfully outlined, the slender flanks are beautifully shaped and the limbs are joined faultlessly to the trunk. The grace of this figure and the *serenity* of its pose [italics added] have never been surpassed, nor have the feet, the hands and the head, whose harmonious proportions and loveliness are in keeping with the rest. To be sure, anyone who has seen Michelangelo's David has no need to see anything else by any other sculptor, living or dead.

Michelangelo was still alive when all these fine words appeared. He read Vasari's account and acknowledged it with a letter, as well as with an encomiastic sonnet *for* Vasari, which Vasari included in a revised version of the life (published in 1568, after Michelangelo's death). Both the letter and the sonnet—and several other letters from Michelangelo included by Vasari—now seem uncomfortably formal. Michelangelo could hardly have been annoyed by Vasari's extravagance, but he could well have felt that the praise was lacking in something, like what his art was about.

Vasari's description of *David* is a good sample of the lack. This enormous figure is only aesthetically "serene," a perfect physical form at rest except for a curious crook in the right wrist, which has caused great critical unrest for centuries. (Is David simply preparing to use his sling?) There is no question about David's facial expression. It is not serene but troubled, a feature of the work that Vasari wholly overlooked. (Of the face he said merely that to satisfy a stupid critic Michelangelo pretended to make a slight change in the nose, after the figure was otherwise complete.) Why troubled? Anyone setting out to fight Goliath had reason to be troubled, and perhaps that simple explanation is enough to suggest a dimension to Michelangelo's thinking neglected by Vasari, who did not worry about the predicaments perfect forms get into. But following Freud's lead, modern critics have of course gone a good bit further. One critic has sensibly proposed that Michelangelo personally identified with David— though he neglects, as Freud would not have, the sexual reverberations of a sculptor identifying with a perfect, 17-foot-high, male figure.* Such approaches to art can be wildly irrelevant to the art, but ignoring the expressive depths of a *David* is a sure way to irrelevance too.

Vasari's real problem was that he did not *want* his artists to be, as David was, disturbed, and in defense of his handling of Michelangelo it should be said that Michelangelo's official commissions, in Florence and the Vatican, were undertaken for officials who did not like disturbances either. As art patrons the latter were good Veblenian specimens looking for showpieces, and so they were amazed and pleased with Michelangelo's "perfection"—though a few of them complained of excessive nudity. From the accounts that I have read I gather that the establishment-patron view of art and artists must have been indistinguishable from Vasari's. Artists could be a bit morose and temperamental without censure, and could have imperfect private lives, but they were expected to produce unambiguously glorified images of the flesh. (A modern equivalent is Soviet poster art.) In other words the faithfulness-to-the-flesh of which they approved was an idealized flesh, always a "selection" of "the most beautiful," and in

---

* Charles Seymour, Jr., offers a psychoanalytic interpretation in his *Michelangelo's David: A Search for Identity.* Unlike Freud, Seymour works from outside evidence, but the evidence is good—a statement in verse by Michelangelo himself in which David's bow is compared with the sculptor's own bow (also a sculpting tool). Seymour also discusses who or what was Michelangelo's Goliath. The remarks make much more personal sense than Vasari's easy assertion that David was a symbol of freedom for Florence, but the chief point is that David had a *struggle* on his hands. Vasari makes him an assured god.

it the idealizing process pretty well displaced spirit. The representa-
tion made no gesture inward, was never suggestive of unresolved
depths.

Michelangelo was an old man when Vasari's first edition came
out, and "little Giorgio" would probably have been too young, anyway, to have been Michelangelo's confidante. Was anyone? There had
been a handsome young man, when Michelangelo was in his fifties,
and after that a lady of high rank to whom he wrote sonnets. Then
there was, Vasari reported, a "servant" who lived with him for years
and to whom he left a large sum of money. But Michelangelo was
certainly a man who liked his privacy, and it would have taxed the wits
of a modern biographer to get close to the "real" man. His letters to
Vasari—quoted in full by Vasari—were wholly friendly and encour-
aging, but they were also uninformative about the self behind them.
Vasari was not the kind of biographer who would have noticed.

After Michelangelo's death Vasari made two additions to his first-
edition account. One was a real stab at moving inward, and the other
was the opposite, an effort to be an establishment man's establishment man about him.

First, he did stingily what Boswell was to do at incredible length
with Samuel Johnson two centuries later. He quoted at seeming random a series of remarks by Michelangelo that he had "made note of,"
intending to show that Michelangelo was patient, modest, and "judicious in all he said," and also "usually profound" as well as "capable
of shrewd and witty pleasantries." The quoting was an excellent
thought, but it was weakened by Vasari's encomiastic urge to select
model quotes. He ended up illustrating Michelangelo's virtues largely
with clever put-downs, such as Michelangelo remarking to an overly
piously dressed cleric, "It would be good for your soul if you were as
good within as you seem to be outside." Such remarks were no better
"within" than the cleric. They were the remarks of a public man being
public. Vasari was not ready—and probably no biographer before
Boswell was ready—to entertain the Boswellian notion that *anything* a
really great man says is worth putting down.

Second, Vasari quoted at much too great length the formal remarks of the great ones in charge of the obsequies for Michelangelo,
such as the pompous Duke Cosimo. Vasari clearly could not see that
such formal remarks were wholly conventional, and could have been
made about persons with nothing like Michelangelo's lustre. Nor
could he see the weakness in using another encomiastic device, oddly

borrowed from the hagiographers: his pious report that after Michel-angelo had been dead twenty-five days his coffin was opened (it had been carried to Florence from Rome with great bureaucratic tedium), and the corpse was "still perfect in every part"—as saints' pure bodies in those days were frequently claimed to be—"and so free from any evil odor that we were tempted to believe that he was merely sunk in a sweet and quiet sleep."

In contrast he disposed of Uccello's death and accomplishments in two or three sentences, mentioning his presumed last words about the rewards of perspective, and adding, with unusual irony, that the rewards—that is, poverty and neglect—had been shared since Uccel-lo's death by artists with similar interests. Uccello was just not Vasa-ri's dish, and what Vasari failed to see in Uccello was at least as limit-ing as what he failed to see in Michelangelo, though of course more evident. Uccello, he was unhappy to report, was deeply "disturbed" not only within, but also right on the canvas. Uccello did not repre-sent "beautifully shaped" flanks. He did not even favor nudes, much less those with "faultlessly joined limbs." His figures gravitated in-stead toward lump, and "the older he grew," said Vasari, "the worse he drew." In art history terms Uccello's obsession with perspective made him a formalist rather than a realist. His formalism put his hu-mans at a disadvantage in their surroundings, which were forbid-dingly symmetrical and cold. Popes and dukes—and therefore Vasari—were not taken by such dissent from opulent, upper-class being. So Uccello was simply judged to be off the track, always "choking his mind with difficult problems," forgetting the essentials of beauty and "doing violence to his nature by fanatical studies."

Interestingly, Ruskin later took the same line, saying that Uccello "went off his head with his love of perspective." The notion of an other-than-serene ambiance surrounding a model body was appar-ently as disturbing to him as that of a model body thinking, like David, unserene thoughts. Even Ruskin was not ready for the coming distortions of modernity. Uccello was indeed a special case.

Of course, Vasari liked to imagine that he could be generous-spir-ited, even about an Uccello. He tried and tried to be open-minded, but usually managed not to be. "Most persons," he once observed of average, imperfect humans, "had in their temperament a touch of uncouthness and even madness that made them outlandish and ec-centric; the dark shadows of vice were often more evident in their lives than the shining light of the virtues that can make men immortal." If only he had been able to see the contradiction in calling "most persons . . . outlandish and eccentric"!

With his emphasis on the perfect and the immortal, he was at one with the hagiographers, but he would have denied the connection. The artists that he and the establishment around him favored at the time were strongly opposed to the abstract religious painting still to be found in the churches, the flat, posed pieces that Vasari called "Byzantine absurdities." Michelangelo had brought "reality" to Christian piety, but Vasari managed to praise that while excluding the mundane, the troubled, and the frail, thus establishing himself as yet another purifier. Also, his steady focus on art rather than artist was quite like the hagiographers' exclusionary preoccupation with soul. In both cases the soul and the body somehow lived miles apart.

IV

Chronicles, Holinshed, Shakespeare —and Breaking Out

From its beginnings the chronicle as a form was tied to officialdom, and particularly to the principle of orderly succession of rulers. After the Fall of Rome, there was no such succession in Italy; officialdom's files in Italy were in a great wastebasket. So, for chroniclers, England was healthier ground, and the climactic result was Raphael Holinshed, several thousand pages of him, and his collaborator Harrison.

Holinshed had two still commonly mentioned forebears, though there were many others. The first was the Venerable Bede (673-735), whose *History of the English Church and People* was prelude to the Holinshed kind of encyclopedism. Bede simply sat down in his monastery (or perhaps he stood up at one of those high, lectern-type desks?) and chronicled the whole known world, beginning right at the beginning. The beginning did not take long, and after he was done with it he had time to put down a physical description of the not yet British Isles, together with their flora, fauna, and inhabitants, before entering on the history he had sources for, and sailing through to his own time.

He must have been venerable at the age of ten to take on so much, yet he wrote many other works in his long life, and also did translations of most of the Old and New Testaments. He was not primarily a biographer, but on the side he turned out three brief encomiastic biographies of church contemporaries. Also, he thought of the chronicle form itself as heavily biographical—being devoted to the lives of kings and saints—so he is certainly a thematic ancestor of Holinshed.

We know more about Bede than about anyone else in Britain in his time, partly because he wrote a little *about* himself, and partly because his chronicle is pleasantly personal. He must have been a splendid man: scholarly, gentle, cautious, but powerfully committed, and, of course, indefatigable. He grew up among churchmen who were worldly and well-traveled (his first teacher visited Rome seven times), and he was surrounded by the classical lore needed for understanding the early Christian Church. Put in the hands of the Church at the age of seven, "ordained deacon at the age of nineteen, and priest at the age of thirty," he naturally wrote of Britain as a Christian world, a missionary world, a Church world. And he also naturally made the core of his history the story of the early missionaries' triumph over paganism. His chronicle was of how saints such as Columba and Augustine were created, how the Gospel was spread, how good kings were baptized and bad ones driven to violent error—all in chronological order, and blessed by Church officialdom. With Bede at the helm, there was no confusion of chronicler intent. He shared with officialdom a clear and simple theory of history: Britain and the world were being steadily nudged upward by their Christian faith.

Like Plutarch, though, Bede also liked truth, as he saw it. He was an honest scholar. He looked around him and found temporary roadblocks to the success of the upward-bound theory, and these prevented him from projecting simple salvation for the gracious at the end of his chronicle. He had to admit that though bishops were abounding and missionary work was proceeding, there had been two strange comets in the sky in the year 729, followed by violence in Gaul and Northumbria. He thought it "impossible to know what to write about [such events], or what the outcome [would] be." He devoutly wished to impose his theory upon history, but he was not a whole-hearted fabulist, even though he had the usual medieval notions of how the natural world worked:

In Ireland there are no reptiles, and no snake can exist there, for although often brought over from Britain, as soon as the ship nears land they breathe its scented air and die. In fact, almost everything in this island enjoys immunity to poison, and I have heard that folk suffering from snake-bite have drunk water in which the scrapings from leaves of books from Ireland [old poems by Yeats perhaps?] have been steeped, and that this remedy checked the spreading poison.

His church conditioning, his devoutness, and the superstitions he shared with his age made him less independent as an historian than his secular successors. Yet hundreds of years later Holinshed and the genre of chronicle were still indebted to him.

The other commonly mentioned early chronicle is *The Anglo-Saxon Chronicle*. King Alfred is said to have started it in the ninth century, though Asser's biography of Alfred does not mention it. Like Bede's church history, it began at the beginning of things, then moved to the beginning of British things, and finally (about page 15) moved to ages in which the scribes—there were many—had a few facts to work with. The early entries were short:

year   1—Octavian reigned 66 years and in the 52nd year of his reign Christ was born.

year   6—five thousand two hundred years had passed from the beginning of the world to this year.

year 33—in this year Christ was crucified, five thousand two hundred and twenty-six years from the beginning of the world.

year 410—in this year the Goths stormed Rome and the Romans never afterwards reigned in Britain.

The scribes recorded the births and deaths of kings, as well as the dates of baptisms, battles, and eclipses. Erratically they mixed in miscellaneous, undirected commentary, sometimes comic:

year 891—in this year . . . three Scots came to King Alfred in a boat without any oars from Ireland, which they had left secretly, because they wished for the love of God to be in foreign lands, they cared not where.

Occasionally the entries came straight from hagiographers:

year 799—in this year the Romans cut out Pope Leo's tongue and put out his eyes and banished him from his see; and then immediately afterward he could, with God's help, see and speak and was again pope as he had been before.

Objections to the scribes' practice of saying ''in this year,'' as well as to their lapses into fantasy-fiction, may have been behind the complaints (about *all* chronicles) issued by the determinedly factual *Encyclopaedia Britannica* in its eleventh edition:

Chronicles are accounts generally of an impersonal character, and often anonymous, composed in varying proportions of passages reproduced textually from sources which the chronicler is seldom at pains to indicate, and of personal recollections the veracity of which remains to be determined. Some of them are written with so little intelligence and spirit that one is led to regard the work of composition as a piece of drudgery imposed on clergy and monks by their superiors.

Bede was neither impersonal nor unintelligent—and he made something of an issue of acknowledging sources. But the monk-transcribers behind the *Anglo-Saxon Chronicle* (several generations' worth) were a mixed crew, not uniformly possessed of scholarly tastes and intentions. And though they all were bearers of the Church's commitments, some were also capable of lapsing into patriotic gore:

> year 937—In this year King Athelstan, lord of nobles, dispenser of treasure to men, and his brother also, Edmund Atheling, won by the sword's edge undying glory in the battle around Brunanburh. The field grew dark with the blood of men, from the time when the sun, that glorious luminary, the bright candle of God, of the Lord eternal, moved over the earth in the hours of the morning, until that noble creation sank at its setting.

For the future of biography, the best passage in the *Anglo-Saxon Chronicle* was on William the Conqueror; it must have been written by someone who knew William well. Unlike any other passage in the work, it reached for the kind of balanced judgment Plutarch admired, describing William as "gentle to the good men who loved God, and stern beyond all measure to those people who resisted his will." A controlling intelligence, not a drudge, wrote it, and achieved a tribute to William that was also a preview of English royal legends to come (think of "a little touch of Harry in the night"):

> Among other things the good security he [William] made in this country is not to be forgotten—so that any honest man could travel over his kingdom without injury with his bosom full of gold; and no one dared strike or kill another, however much wrong he had done him. And if any man had intercourse with a woman against her will, he was forthwith castrated.

But writing in praise of William was not enough for this writer. He also had the independence and freedom (as Holinshed did later, living outside church walls) to be *critical* of his hero. Speaking as a member of the unmoneyed class, he was especially hard on William's fiscal practices. William oppressed the poor, he said, and overtaxed them; and sometimes he showed more kindness for his harts and boars than for his underlings. Worse,

Into avarice did he fall,
And loved greediness above all.

Official records have not been noted for rushing to criticize their officials, but the *Anglo-Saxon Chronicle* was such a mishmash that anything could be found in it. Its precedent was confusing but probably healthy.

◆ ◆

Raphael Holinshed was and was not official, but he was a predictable, reliable, quite remarkable scholar-mole and patriot-pedant. We know next to nothing about him, and scholarly interest in him has been limited to little pieces in his *Chronicles* that Shakespeare found useful. So his importance as an historian in his own right has gone largely unrecognized, and as a biographer ignored. Publication of his monster work in 1577–78 was made possible by the invention of print—monks would have despaired of copying it—but that work was backed by hundreds of years of English historicity from Bede on, years that had given the country its language and its royal tradition, as well as its national church. Holinshed inhaled the whole of this past, but he also had views, which he expressed. Like Bede, he was quite his own man in the chronicle world.

His work ran to millions of words, a true wonder of labor comparable to the fat encyclopedias to come. One of the few students of the whole of it, Stephen Booth, observes that it is equal in length to the Old and New Testaments, all of Shakespeare, *War and Peace*, and a few other items rolled into one. He also claims that thirteen Shakesperean plays are drawn from it, and though I can vouch only for *Macbeth*, *Lear*, *Richard II*, *Henry IV* (1 and 2), and *Henry V*, those six are enough to show Shakespeare's debt.

The game for a student of Shakespeare is to see how Shakespeare *molded* chronicle materials into drama, and sometimes to speculate about other, additional sources he may have used. In the case of *King Lear*, for instance, there seems to have been, besides Holinshed, a now-missing popular Elizabethan play, also called *King Lear*.* For *Macbeth*, on the other hand, Holinshed provided *all* the major plot ingredients, as well as Shakespeare's assumptions about the characters of Macbeth and his Lady. So comparing Holinshed with Shakespeare's *Macbeth* seems easy until it becomes evident that Shakespeare borrowed from four widely separate passages in Holinshed. Seeing the master at his patchwork is broadening but also deceiving. The transformational process was radically creative.

Holinshed was reticent about himself in the *Chronicles*, but not about the plan for their creation. In a preface, dedicated with promotional intent to England's Chancellor of the Exchequer, he said that he had begun the work under assignment to a loyal, hard-working English subject by the name of Reginald Wolfe, "late printer to the Queenes Majesty." Wolfe had meant "to publish an universal cosmography of the whole world," but had thought of the chronicle side of it later, a mere addition of the "particular histories of every known nation." He had assigned a relative of his, Harrison, the cosmography, and had given Holinshed the histories. Then this ambitious Wolfe died, leaving Harrison and Holinshed to cut his immensities down to only three hundred thousand words of cosmography (with none of the maps that printer Wolfe had planned) and three million words of history.

The three million words of history were confined to England, Scotland, and Ireland, and dealt, one by one, with all the rulers there for a thousand years.

Harrison had a preface of his own for the cosmography, which he dedicated to a patron, Sir William Brooke, telling him that he, Harrison, was personally very sedentary for one expected to cover so much ground: "Until now of late, except it were from the parish where I dwell, unto your Honour in Kent or out of London, where I was born unto Oxford and Cambridge, where I have been brought up, I never travelled 40 miles forthright and at one journey in my life." Harrison went on to describe himself as a bookish minister who sat close to a hearth with a great many tomes, some "utterly mangled and defaced

---

* The Lear story is a pleasant short fable in the *Chronicles*, a cameo with a happy ending. Lear returns from France with Cordelia to defeat the bad sisters and retake his throne.

with wet," and pasted together his geography like a schoolboy at the town library (he even had a chart of distances between towns). To the geography he added, with no seeming hardship, a "brief rehearsal" of "the nature and qualities of the people of England, and such commodities as are to be found in the same."

Holinshed's own pasting may have been like this. Encyclopedic combinings were what both men had in mind, not pioneering scholarship, but they were at least conscientious in listing their sources (about one hundred fifty going back to Caesar's *Commentaries*). They of course cited many other chronicles, as well as district registers and records, but interestingly no accounts of saints, not even Aelfric's. They did mention the Catholic martyr Edmund Campion, an inclusion that may not have pleased Queen Elizabeth.*

Both Holinshed and Harrison thought of themselves modestly as anthologists of known materials, and this has been the opinion passed down about their work. It was, after all, a work that was begun by an ambitious printer anxious to show the world what quantitative wonders print could accomplish. Yet their modesty is misleading. Both Harrison and Holinshed controlled and commented on their materials, and should definitely be thought of as historians (and biographers), not patchers. They were masters at selecting and shaping the best material at hand, and at converting it into an orderly whole. There was no fragmentation in their work, no obvious piecing, and there were no grand gaps. There was elegant coherence within paragraphs, and from one paragraph to another, a coherence reinforced by a marginal gloss that summarized the narrative. There was also intelligent attention to the overall order of chapters and books, with each section summarized in a lengthy heading. There was even an index.

The work was crammed with opinions, some of which had the air of official doctrine, some not. Holinshed was definitely a man for editorials, and was free with them. His chief officialness stemmed from his royalism. He was faithful to the principle of royalty as a system possessed of divine legitimacy, and he could put up with much in its defense. With an inept king like Richard II he was in trouble, but could be depended on to have a positive opinion in the end. First he

---

* A second or third edition of the *Chronicles* (1587) included a life of Elizabeth (not written by Holinshed) that was heavily censored, but passages about Campion's execution had been excised.

was fair to Richard's critics, summarizing their accounts of his extravagance and venality at length—how he fed ten thousand persons daily at his court, with "yeomen and groomes . . . clothed in silks . . . oversumptuous ye may be sure for their estates"; and how he preferred "lewd and most vaine persons" to "bishoprikes," and permitted within his "plentiful house . . . the filthy sinne of lecherie and fornication, with abhominable adulterie." But then he turned around and, while not refuting the critics, declared that Richard had been "a prince the most unthankfullie used of his subjects of any one of whom ye shall lightlie read." Holinshed's final position on Richard was essentially York's in Shakespeare's *Richard II*, and Holinshed was if anything more loyal to Richard than Shakespeare was.

It was in this balanced but editorially firm manner that Holinshed judged all his kings as he plodded through them. His manner was Plutarchian, and though he brought to it much strong nationalism, his debt to Plutarch's tradition of the high, serious, and public remained great. Also, despite his nationalism, his assessments were wholly his own, and therefore sometimes deviationist. He was not sold on the *inevitable* rightness of royalty, nor on its mystical trappings. He had obviously read Machiavelli, and could tell a hawk from a handsaw, public piety from earnest intent. As a conscientious historian, he culled his sources, especially in reporting on the ceremonious in royal lives.

The Renaissance was a time of ceremonies, and of the pageantry that went with them—the dress, the emblems, the paraphernalia, and the rhetoric. But for Holinshed the ceremonious was not of interest unless it revealed something about the characters and events behind it. Take coronations. They had become posh long before Elizabeth, but had not always been so. When Alfred was made king there was apparently no coronation at all. Said Asser (and no more), "Alfred took over the government of the whole kingdom as soon as his brother [Ethelred] died, with the approval of the divine will and according to the unanimous wish of all the inhabitants of the kingdom."

After Alfred, the rites of both church and state grew more clotted. Christianity became a bureaucracy, and royalty became a bureaucracy mixed with Christian bureaucracy, thereby doubling the necessary knee-bending for governmental change (one could no longer ask for a show of hands, take over, and go fight the Danes). Pomp is like red tape, a diversionary necessity bred by excessive government, and Holinshed well understood it. He could not avoid mentioning the anointings and crownings, but he did so selectively and to serve his own purposes. For King John's coronation he printed verbatim the text of a tribute written by the Archbishop of Canterbury—which said that John was "a person of high prowesse and no less prudence" —but then hurried to point out that John had in fact established a political spoils system, and had made the Archbishop Lord Chancellor in return for the Archbishop's kind words. (Holinshed underlined the point by adding that the Archbishop "gloried in the honour whereto he was preferred" and loved "worldlie pomp.")

With Richard II's coronation, on the other hand, Holinshed dwelt at length on the pomp, on the ostentation and frippery of the occasion, including the presence of four beautiful virgins, "of stature and age like the king," who threw gold coins at him as he approached, to show that it was Richard himself who was led by frippery. Then, with Henry IV, he shifted focus again, dismissing all the coronation ceremonies, rushing on (as Shakespeare was also to do with Henry IV) to the intrigue underneath them.

Holinshed's handling of Henry IV is especially striking, since we can compare it with the account of the coronation by one of his peers and regular sources, the French chronicler Froissart. Froissart went on for pages about the ceremony, describing Henry in "a short cote of cloth of gold . . . mounted on a white courser" passing by "seven conduits running with wine, white and a red," and lords "in their furs of robes of scarlet, furred with menyver." Froissant also dealt at length with such customary observances as that of asking if anyone were present to challenge the king's right to the crown. Holinshed could readily have pasted all this matter into his own account, but did not.

He had, then, little antiquarian interest in ceremony, and little interest in the symbolism of it either, the aura of significance around maces, scepters, silk damatics, rings, swords, sandals. If he were alive today, he would be a political scientist at, perhaps, Princeton, with the difference that he was in the *ethical* tradition of political reportage, as his modern successors are not, the tradition that all my subjects here, from Plutarch on, lived with and accepted.

I mean that he conceived of his chronicles as, beyond chronicling, moral instruments. He could be oddly Swiftian in recognizing the human norm of "subversion of peoples, desolation of provinces . . . and other lamentable accidents diversely happening upon sundry occasions." But he always wished that his reader would "reap fruit" from all that, particularly from the evidence of how his leader-models performed in the wicked world. His stance was definitely Plutarch's. He could be depended upon to move from the evidence to the lessons to be learned, lessons at the heart of the old biography, lessons in virtue.

Such lessoning obviously limited his independence as a thinker. He would never have undertaken his work if he had not been a strong royalist, Christian, and patriot. He took usurpation and illegitimacy of rule as moral problems with mystical, suprapolitical dimensions. He gave Shakespeare his pieties for the play sequence *Richard II*, *Henry IV* (1 and 2), and *Henry V*, making it a history of a primal sin followed by repentance, conversion, and, eventually, national salvation. The parallel between this pattern of action and the hagiographers' was oddly close, and in both cases the results were theme-led histories. Holinshed was a hard-history man in the morning, but in the afternoon he went to church.

Shakespeare accepted but moderated such piety, and we should not make too much of his debt to the great chronicler. With the mysterious ingredients of human character—particularly character in private, character when not enthroned—Shakespeare was his own man.

♦ ♦

And now I come to that man himself. Perhaps he should not be here at all. He has no status as a biographer, and for centuries the literary professionals have had their hands full just dealing with him in his announced genres. He borrowed characters from Plutarch and Holinshed, but he took the usual stage liberties with them in doing so, putting words in the mouths of kings and nobles that not even biographers invented. His place was the theater. He made the kings and nobles over into theater—not a proper role for a biographer. A biographer is not supposed to be so free.

Yet we have seen biographers being so free—even, say, Aelfric. Aelfric was an honest, scholarly monk, and made a point of being faithful to his (dubious) sources, but he had no qualms about making his "lives" over into instructive weekly homilies.

And we have also seen the tradition of biography impinged upon, and contributed to, by the nonbiographers Machiavelli and Cellini. Shakespeare may not have been a biographer, but he was a greater force for change in biography than they, perhaps even a greater force for change than any biographer with a right to be *called* biographer, until Boswell. It is tiresome to go about muttering about his greatness, but there he is.

Or was. But what was he? As far as biography is concerned, he was a great playwright whose approach to character on stage made his audience think of character off stage, made his hearers wonder— though perhaps they should not have—how many children Lady Macbeth had, and whether or not Hamlet had an Oedipus complex. The long history of Shakespearean commentary has been steadily a battleground between those who have been so attracted to his characters that they have removed them from the stage for study and companionship, and those who have been furious about the removal. He must have done something big to have started the battle in the first place.

What he did has been described in many ways, but seems always to have been related to his discomfort within the literary and dramatic conventions that were his livelihood. They bothered him. He kept leaving them and walking out in the air. The result was excellent for the conventions—they needed the air—but it happened to be good for biography too. The stage time was as cluttered with kings and nobles as early biography was, and as restricted by their pomp and circumstance. Shakespeare must have discovered early, probably with *Richard II*, how hard it was to find the human in the words and actions of *enthroned* humans. Luckily, his stage was also receptive to other than kings and nobles, as biography (if we exclude artists and saints) was not. The fusions and confusions of rank and role in Elizabethan drama were behind Polonius's recital of what the players in *Hamlet* were expert in: "tragedy, comedy, history, or pastoral, pastoral-comical, tragical-historical, tragical-historical-comical-pastoral, scene undividable and poem unlimited." To have been even more comprehensive, Polonius might also have given them expertise in morality-mystery masquery, and puppetry. The stage was a hodge-podge then, a fine chaos that Shakespeare thrived on.

Like the chroniclers, he was an anthologist of sorts, but not of histories only. He was a synthesist of genres, fashions, rhetorics—and therefore also of the high and the low, the grave and the trivial. The ideal "statement" he was reaching for as he effected his mergers cannot be precisely defined, but surely it bore upon making the staged less stagey, or, in biographical terms, making public characters whole. Reading Plutarch and Holinshed, he must have asked himself constantly, How can I convert such an idiotic grandee as Richard, or Henry, or Julius, or Antony, into a person?

Some critics—notably E. E. Stoll—have thought that Shakespeare did *not* ask such a question. They have preferred to keep the playwright at work as a playwright, the stage man constantly on stage. Stoll's position, applied to *Hamlet*, has the final, complicated character of Hamlet emerging from the merely technical problems of timing and suspense that Shakespeare faced as he tried to make a bad old revenge play his own. Thus, in Stoll's view, Shakespeare brought in the psychic-delay motif of the play for the nonpsychic reason that the *old* play had nothing but empty public rhetoric keeping the hero from taking action for several acts. Stoll's thesis is sensible as far as it goes, but it stops so short that it leaves us a Shakespeare who was a stage-effects man, no more.

Stoll knew perfectly well that his thesis stopped short; he stopped short deliberately, in annoyance at all the complications introduced by other critics—Bradleyan, Freudian, Marxist—who would not stop at all. I understand his annoyance, but I still think that Shakespeare would not have settled on the psychic-delay motif if he had not *first* asked how he might make a stupid, merely vengeful character-type into an intelligent and intelligible being.

I insist on the question because it is a biographer's question as much as, maybe more than, a dramatist's; but in insisting I do not mean to make Shakespeare out to be a radical innovator, a rebel among the conventional actors and dramatists around him. Obviously he was not. Like Holinshed, he was a reasonably loyal subject and patriot, a respecter of legitimacy, an establishment Christian, and a smart theatrical entrepreneur. It was his orthodoxy as a young playwright, for instance, that kept him close to Holinshed when he wrote the *Richard II–Henry V* sequence, which was institutional mythology rampant. There he paid every respect to the sinfulness of rebellion against an anointed king, and to the consequences. The solemn mouthings of the great were in all those plays. The pomp was in all those plays. The playwright's commitment in them was a grave one to God, country, and the pieties.

And Shakespeare never gave up this youthful commitment wholly, though he had clear lapses. What he did was learn, from stage experience, that the pieties did not make the grandees live; and learning this he began casting about for remedies.

Basically he found two, both of which are represented, primitively, in the *Richard II–Henry V* sequence. First, he sought to give each grandee a chance to speak as a person rather than as a fixture; and second, he sought to deflate each grandee somehow, to cut him down to size, make him a forked beast when not enthroned. Together the two remedies were a recipe by which to improve both drama and biography.

Richard II is the first and most formal of the Holinshed-derived plays, and *no* deflation occurs in it. Nothing, for instance, could be more formal—or dull—than the conflict between Bolingbroke and Mowbray, for which Shakespeare followed Holinshed dutifully, letting Mowbray call Bolingbroke a false and disloyal traitor at length, and allowing Mowbray to return the insult to the blowing of trumpets. The only deviant moment in the play is not deflationary, but it is at least ostensibly private. In that moment Richard speaks to himself at length in prison, just before his murder. There he compares his prison to the world, populates it with his thoughts, and the thoughts become minutes, the hours groans. As soliloquies go, it is far too brittle, too carefully *worked* to be a credible private event, but it is nonetheless a shift, a beginning. Richard's words and notions at that moment are material the playwright had no historical base for, so they are created out of the air for the obvious, pressing reason that he had to do *something* with a character sitting alone in a cell preparing for death. Do what? He had to have him *think*.

Holinshed never thought of having his characters think. History, it seemed then, had no stake in thought.

In the later plays of the *Richard II–Henry V* sequence there were other soliloquies, but the big advance in these plays was the introduction of Falstaffian horseplay, also taboo in chronicles. The horseplay ranged widely, but was most relevantly deflationary when Prince Hal and Falstaff took turns playing king. Those great scenes should not be called comic relief—"relief" points in the wrong direction—but straight satire, analysis, criticism of the grave chronicle mode. They directly addressed the frailties of public pomp itself.

But they did so without changing history. A playwright cannot allow a Falstaff—wise though he may be—to run history. So Shakespeare disposed of Falstaff in *Henry IV* (2), and in *Henry V* went back to the Holinshed solemnities.

The same can be said, I think, of Shakespeare's first play out of Plutarch. *Julius Caesar* has a good moment when Brutus reveals his dream life as a prospective murderer (interestingly, Plutarch supplied the moment). It also has Antony briefly stepping out of his public character (following his "Friends, Romans, Countrymen" speech) and saying, "Villainy, thou art afoot." Otherwise the play is thoroughly in the public tradition.

Neither Holinshed nor Plutarch led Shakespeare where he went with *Hamlet* and *King Lear*, however. They may even have inhibited him as he proceeded, since the step he took with character in the great tragedies required the freedom of the fabulous, the freedom of *not* being tied to historical familiars. A misty, mythical early Denmark and a rainy, mythical early Britain proved useful.

Developing the characters of Hamlet and Lear gave Shakespeare a chance both to undermine the gravity of kingship and to allow his heroes to think. As he moved from one to the other—the two plays were separated by five years of stage history—he managed to display the whole range of character, as popularized in our time by David Riesman, between the inner- and other-directed self. Hamlet is an introvert whose depths have attracted dozens of psychoanalysts. Lear is the opposite. He has no soliloquies, and even in his dying moments directs our attention not to himself but to Cordelia. Hamlet and Lear are the north and south poles of tragic heroism, and while Shakespeare may have just happened on their difference, just happening on things has always been the way of genius.

When we think of the character Hamlet, we think first of his soliloquies, the meditative cast of the man, his inwardness. And connected with his inwardness we think of how his thoughts about himself produced irresoluteness, doubt, mystery. Especially mystery. The words that finally best apply to him were his own, when he complained of those who did seek to know him:

How unworthy a thing you make of me.
You would play upon me; you would seem to know my stops;
You would pluck out the heart of my mystery.

Yet for all his solemnity, Hamlet was also the play's and Shakespeare's wittiest wit, with as many one-liners as any comic in the whole canon. He combined his wit with moral severity, castigating all the play's hypocrites and Machiavellians, yet the wit remained wit, and funny too. He was his own fool, a zany, "your only jig maker," replying to no one except Horatio without a barb, a verbal twist. And with each witticism, he added to his depth, meanwhile walking around in black and being the gravest figure of the play.

Lear, on the other hand, had, as his fool said, only a tiny little wit, was not introspective, and spent no time at all debating with himself about what he should do. In fact, his right to make decisions about himself was taken from him entirely for four of the five acts. He became a sufferer, not an enactor. He took his cues, then, not from Aristotelian tragedy, which required that he be responsible for his fall, but from comedy, the comedy of the low, the comedy of those who have learned to seek only survival, not justice.

In our time Lear's kind of predicament appears in the comedy of Beckett. Poor Lear, even when most mad, could not quite learn the survival philosophy of the low, but he came close. His was a remarkable education for a grandee. He even discovered that he was not to be granted final purification and redemption, and went to his death saying "Never, never, never, never, never"—probably the most frightening line in Shakespeare.

The unredeemed death of Lear makes the play the severest deviation from traditional tragedy that Shakespeare attempted. Note how conventional his Hamlet's end in comparison, as he rises to "felicity." Yet Hamlet rather than Lear has been the attractive character for modern audiences. For us Hamlet is a *case*. He is a neurotic troubled by difficult decisions, hence a believable human. Lear is not a case, but a pawn in a system that is a case. Therefore *King Lear* is a great play, but *Hamlet* is a great play with a great character in it. And perhaps on this point even Aristotle would have agreed, having once decreed that "character is that which reveals moral purpose, showing the kinds of things a man chooses or avoids."

Yet I must insist that Lear is in his way equally credible, equally whole in his humanity. Character is not character solely when it makes choices—such as to kill or not to kill King Claudius at prayer—and there is ruling-class blindness built into Aristotle's (and Plutarch's and some modern psychologists') insistence that choice is crucial. Aristotle's grave minds were minds in charge of their destinies, and the minds he thought trivial were not. Yet many great figures in comedy have shown us depths of understanding not approached by lofty choosers. The comic souls have learned not to choose but to survive.

There is a comic way, sometimes a black comic way, into character (and therefore biography) that opens up as soon as the principle of choice is simply removed. Think of Sancho. With Lear, Shakespeare was working on the Sancho way.

I must mention one other step that Shakespeare took in breaking out of the conventions he inherited. He took it particularly in *Macbeth* and *Measure for Measure*, and took it with the vigor of someone annoyed but suppressed by surrounding moral imperatives. Chronologically, *Macbeth* and *Measure for Measure* sit between *Hamlet* and *King Lear*. Both are superficially conformist to their genres, and both are what we would today call exposés. They are exposés of model leaders. And both are studies, really remarkable for their time, of obsessions.

Like Hamlet, Macbeth is inner directed (though he has ample help from his Lady), but unlike Hamlet, he is directed to do rather than not do, and the directing becomes uncontrollable. A "dagger of the mind" has him and "marshall'st him" where he is going. He who comes before us at the beginning of the play as a model leader, an ethical leader, loses control of himself and cannot be diverted from carrying through with the "imperial theme" at any cost. The result is that the theme—which is one of public service, public trust—turns on him, turns to evil.

Similarly, Angelo, put in a place of power because of his integrity and purity, finds his purity turning against him, filling his life with paradox as he plots impurities with the purest of females and sentences other impure ones to death. The good (and improbable) duke of *Measure for Measure* save the play from being a tragedy, and Shakespeare allows Angelo, as he did not allow Macbeth, to repent. But in both plays the damage to the fetish of moral public leadership is what lingers. Both Macbeth and Angelo are sick men, and their sickness is given to us as a product of their apparent moral superiority.

Their obsessions are of a kind much studied in modern leaders, and memorably pointed up by a pioneer in modern biography, Lytton Strachey, who displays the underpinnings of the noble religious and moral drives of Cardinal Manning and Florence Nightingale as excessive, out of control, fanatical. Classical writers never handled frailty thus. They thought not of sickness but of ethics. A frailty was something that one could (and should) choose not to submit to.

◆ ◆

Starting with Plutarch, the assumptions behind the biographical writings discussed so far have been uniformly close to those declared by Aristotle to be proper for a tragic hero, close even when the subject was a saint, close even when the subject was Machiavellian (for such a person had, ideally, moral public ends); so that to study early tragedy is also to study early biography, or the main ingredients thereof. In one way or another all the biographical writers I have mentioned did accept an ethical-model theory of character as the basis for writing biography at all. It is precisely because the connection between tragedy and biography was so close that Shakespeare's breaking out of the pattern of tragedy has bearing. What he brought to tragedy made, and still makes, ripples beyond the stage.

Along with his questioning of the ethical pattern he introduced a skepticism about the importance and meaning of leadership itself that would have offended Aristotle and the rest. It was not that he gave up on leaders as proper subjects for tragedy, but rather that he questioned the credibility of elements of the leader myths he worked. No one in tragedy or biography had ever thought to do that, though the writers of comedy had. Shakespeare himself came to it slowly but, with *Hamlet* and the later plays, decisively.

Before *Hamlet* he had too many obligations to the kingship theme to be fully diverted, but with *Hamlet* the bud of discontent blossomed in him. He created a Hamlet who doubted that the slings and arrows of leadership and revenge were worthwhile, a Lear who came to wish to be out of it all with Cordelia, a Cleopatra who disdained Roman thoughts, a Timon who went down to the sea to gnaw at roots, and even a Prospero who became at last petulant and unpleasant about being responsible. *Not* to be a leader, *not* to live up to snuff, was hardly a new idea, but it was certainly an idea biography had been waiting for. And what Shakespeare helped do was implant the idea in the minds of the leader-models themselves.

We go to the garden for food, to the well for water. We come back from the garden and well and we eat and drink. We do this for our whole lives, and the doing is what sustains us for our whole lives, being one basic kind of life meaning—a daily meaning, a continuum of low, mean, but not trivial meaning—unto death.

Of all the human arts, biography and autobiography are the chief ones—except the arts of physical sustenance, such as gardening and cooking—with generic cause to *render* that meaning. It was odd, then, but crucial, that biography should have grown up with tragedy, and shaped itself in that world. And it was odd as well, and also crucial, that Shakespeare (working himself up to his own brand of tragedy) should have grown up with biography—that is, with Plutarch and Holinshed and other chroniclers. He was not a radical, and in the theater he was working with genres that could tolerate only limited sprawl. But he was also working, he found out early, with lives. Roughly half of his plays are essentially dramatized historical lives, lives of the high born, lives of the grave. The traditions of early biography as well as tragedy are deep in them.

And so it is a clear mark of his genius that Shakespeare could take these traditions and move out and away from them. The genius of it has been well described by Friedrich Nietzsche. Nietzsche is a villain now, and shows up on our twentieth-century screen as a sort of Edmund, but in the following remarks (which take their impulse from Hamlet's friendly comment to Horatio on the limits of his philosophy) he gives an uncharacteristically gentle appraisal of the impurities of Shakespeare's art, with its mixture of traditional, disciplined uplift and plain dailiness:

> The essential thing "in heaven and earth" is, apparently, that there should be long obedience in the same direction; there thereby results, and has always resulted in the long run, something which has made life worth living: for instance, virtue, art, music, dancing, reason, spirituality—*anything* [italics added] that is transfiguring, refined, foolish or divine. The communicability of ideas, the discipline which the thinker imposed upon himself to think in accordance with the rules of a church or a court, or conformable to Aristotelian premises, the persistent spiritual will to interpret everything that happened according to a Christian scheme, and in every occurrence to rediscover and justify the Christian god:—all this violence, arbitrariness, severity, dreadfulness and unreasonableness has proved itself the disciplinary means whereby the European spirit has attained its strength, its remorseless curiosity and subtle mobility; granted also that much irrecoverable strength had to be stifled, suffocated and spoiled in the process.

V

Samuel Johnson

S amuel Johnson (1709–1784) could not have been the first interesting biographical subject who ever lived, but we have so much
information about him that it is easy to think the genre began with
him. We should be happy that he was interesting, but not happy, I
think, with the quantity of print that has come of the interest. Since
Johnson's time no literary form has equaled biography in the squirrel-
ing of incidental material like old bills and hatbands, and no literary
form has achieved greater formlessness. But it was not Johnson who
started the trend; it was his biographer, James Boswell (1740–1795).

The two men did not meet until Johnson was famous and fifty-
three, and Boswell's account of Johnson's early life has proved to be
endlessly emendable by scholars. Yet Boswell's exhaustive reporting
procedures have been praised even by severe critics, notably Lord
Macaulay. Macaulay said he was "a coxcomb and a bore, weak, vain,
pushing, curious [and] garrulous," but thought he was a good biographer because "everything which another man would have hidden"—
such as Johnson's insults—"was matter of gay and clamorous exulta-
tion to his weak and diseased mind." Boswell himself explained his
thoroughness rather differently, quoting an ancient rabbi who had
said that even the idle talk of a good man ought to be regarded, and
adding that in view of the eminence of his subject, he felt "justified in
preserving rather too many of Johnson's sayings than too few." The
resultant completeness was not to be equaled until the days of the
tape recorder.

How closely would tapes have corroborated Boswell's reporting? We will never know. What we do know is that with the appearance of his work, biography gained a new dimension.

I agree with John Wain that Johnson and Boswell together—two biographers so unlike each other that it is a wonder they became friends—make an historic point of division in the genre's history. Wain's generalization on the point needs qualifications (and his own biography of Johnson is full of them), but it is a good place to begin:

> Boswell was a contemporary of Rousseau, his life overlapped with Byron's. To him, the quirks of individual psychology were of absorbing interest. . . . Johnson is the tail end of the previous epoch, an epoch stretching back three thousand years. To him the most important features of a man's character are those which he shares with the greatest number of other people.

In other words Boswell's *Life of Johnson* was miles away from Johnson's *Lives of the Poets*. Yes, and this was so because Johnson was in debt to the biographical tradition of Plutarch, while Boswell was chiefly in debt to the eccentric genius of Johnson, and to a new world of egocentrism that Johnson was in some ways too old for.

And yet, oddly, Johnson himself contributed—especially in his *Life of Savage*—a great deal to the New World approach to the genre. As evidence of how differently Johnson, an eighteenth-century classicist, viewed biography, compared with the classicists themselves, I recommend his *Rambler* essay (printed in its entirety here as an appendix). In it he sided with Plutarch on the superiority of biography to history, but for the un-Plutarchian reason that it afforded "lessons in the private life." He agreed with Plutarch that "glorious exploits" were sometimes less instructive than "matters of less moment,"* but unlike Plutarch, he proposed that *any* life was a suitable subject, since "we are all prompted by the same motives, all deceived by the same fallacies, all animated by hope, obstructed by danger, entangled by desire, and seduced by pleasure." Unlike Plutarch, he recommended attention to "minute details," but like Plutarch, he saw biography as an occasion for studying the ways to knowledge and virtue. In short his essay, though it is one of the great statements about biography, does not side clearly with either the ancient or the modern school. Johnson was always his own school.

---

* Plutarch, in the opening remarks to his life of Alexander.

But I am ahead of myself. One of the ways of coming at Johnson is to compare a few of the biographies of the man. Courses in comparative Johnsons are taught at our universities, and they are really courses in comparative biography. I do not know how many biographies of him have been written—too many—but to begin with Boswell, move to Macaulay (1856), and then jump to a number of moderns, is to acquire a good sense of what all the fuss has been about. I will refer intermittently to Boswell, Macaulay, and, among the moderns, Joseph Wood Krutch, John Wain, and W. Jackson Bate, as well as to Johnson's own very brief autobiographical account of his birth and early life. The world does not need another Johnson biography from me, but as Macaulay prophesied, interest in the man has come to supersede interest in his works. Then too, for my purposes, the man and his works—particularly the biographies he wrote himself—have to move together, since he was much more personal in his approach to a life than the classical tradition in which he matured sanctioned.

Perhaps he was personal because he was himself personable—in a way that an ugly physical being can be personable—and because his early poverty drove him as a writer to depend upon his own private resources for survival. He became a hack in the days when being a hack—that is, writing on commission, being paid by the piece, or line, or word—was still a novelty. In that age, as Macaulay put it, "literature had ceased to flourish under the patronage of the great, and had not begun to flourish under the patronage of the public." What Macaulay did not mention—for he was not given to qualifications—was that Johnson's greatest feat as a hack was to be at the same time his own man. For many years in the London jungle he drove himself to produce sheer linage (saying, "No man but a blockhead ever wrote, except for money"), but in that time he also earned his reputation as one from whose books all persons might "advance in virtue."

His feat had its roots in his talent for balancings. Rhetorically he was a disciple of Plutarch, always setting one clause against another, and one virtue against one vice. But the rhetorical habit went beyond words in him and seems to have been a part of his psyche from the beginning. As the child of a scholarly bookseller with no head for money, and a pious mother with no head for *thoughts* about piety, he was early driven by familial circumstance to mix literature with bread, and blind faith with his own wide-ranging rational intelligence. Also, as a child born with great physical defects, and an equally great sensibility, he had to learn to live with the ugly strangeness that others saw in him. Macaulay is the biographer who made most of that strangeness, not out of malice but because he was at all times a literary showman and could not miss a chance for a sequence of punch lines; so it was Macaulay who dwelt upon Johnson's "deeply scarred face [from scrofula] . . . his grimaces, his gestures, his mutterings," and did *not* dwell upon his equal capacity for, in appropriate circumstances, grace. Yet it is Macaulay who has to be heard here if we are to understand the duality of the forces inside Johnson, he who "terrified people who did not know him," whom "the sight of food affected . . . as it affects birds of prey," who at a dinner table "would, in a fit of absence, stoop down and twitch off a lady's shoe," or "amaze a drawing room by suddenly ejaculating a clause of the Lord's Prayer." The strangeness of the man made good copy for Macaulay, but it was also a true part of him, and a part that did much to make him unrepresentative of the pre-Romantic ways of literature and biography—not, that is, just a classical intelligence, or just a Tory.

Johnson's physical strangeness must be particularly noted in connection with the purification theme I have been threading through this volume. It was a form of impurity so conspicuous that he could only, when confronted with pretensions of purity in others, be struck by his difference from them. And he *was* struck. His own account of his early life—known as his "annals"—shows a remarkable concentration on the affairs of his private being, containing no general remarks about his family tree, the town of Lichfield, the state of bookselling, or literature in the provinces beyond Grub Street. The plainness of his first two paragraphs was simply not in the spirit of classical gravity, nor was their concentration upon the physical:

> Sept 7, 1709, I was born at Lichfield. My mother had a very difficult and dangerous labour, and was assisted by George Hector, a man-midwife of great reputation. I was born almost dead, and could not cry for some time. When he had me in his arms he said, "Here is a brave boy."
>
> In a few weeks an inflammation was discovered on my buttock, which was, I think, taken for a burn; but soon appeared to be a natural disorder. It swelled, broke, and healed.

The account then proceeded for about a thousand words, up to a paragraph in which the physical was replaced by a five-sentence account of his mother's effort to inform him of a "future state." (It was "a fine place filled with happiness, called Heaven" as well as "a sad place, called Hell.") After this he wrote, for thirty-eight pages, of matters so personal that he later felt obliged to purify them himself, by burning them. Naturally, his modern biographers have enjoyed the missing pages even more than the ones they still have.

Later Johnsonian remarks have dulled the pages' mystery. It now seems clear that he was in later life full of guilt about his early annoyance with his parents, annoyance that he probably recorded in the missing pages. Yet the fact that he burned the pages tells us of the contrariness of the impulses in him: to speak of such matters, and not to.

Modern biographers have shown their own colors about his psychic stresses. Krutch makes much of the moral side of his guilt feelings. Bate psychoanalytically speaks of the "negative image" Johnson had of his father, and of the security he felt with his mother, though not respecting her. And Wain wanders off to speculate about the limitations of parents as parents when their lives are darkened by poverty and struggle. Yet the bare account by Johnson himself, together with the burned pages, seems more informative than any of these.

The burned pages constituted three-fourths of the whole fragmentary manuscript, which only took Johnson up to the age of eleven, and focused on unpleasant memories such as learning Latin verbs and dealing with an uncle who was "a very mean and vulgar man, drunk every night . . . proud and ostentatious but, luckily, not rich." Just one Johnsonian generalization was planted amid such detail: the difficulty of remembering things "read without pleasure." Otherwise the account was so lacking in the kind of eighteenth-century profundity Johnson is famous for that it might have been written by another person in another time.

After his eleventh year and these "annals," his education took place under several schoolmasters of varying merit, and then at Oxford for thirteen months (he could find funds for no more). The elements of it have been pieced together from many sources, but none with the "annals" flavor. Nor do we have accounts—except from others, and from Johnson himself in his more portentous vein—of his marriage to "Tetty" (nearly twice his age), of his failure to make a go at teaching, and of his move to London, age twenty-eight, to learn the arts of survival in the city's writing world. What we do have is the contrast between his writings before London and after.

It is in part a contrast between juvenilia and mature work, but the maturity of his first London productions is not as impressive as the change in his literary intent, from the lofty and distant to the directly journalistic and satiric. In London he had to learn, and learn quickly, how to hack, but he also had to learn to cope with his own solidifying social anger.

The anger got in the way of loftiness. At school he had begun, naturally, as a poet, and as a poet he had dealt with virtue and vice in the abstract manner he found around him. We now have for evidence of his Oxford creations a clumsy poem in couplets called *The Young Author*, in which he cautions a young rustic moving into the big world against letting his idealism lead him to false hopes of fame and glory. The trouble with the cautions is that the poem itself does not heed them; a remote idealism clouds it utterly. Biographer Bate has described the poem as "of remarkable psychological interest," but it seems to me revelatory in only the most vapid, harmless terms—a young romantic trying to be a great realist—since its feelings are thoroughly distanced by the conventional pastoral machinery Johnson was later to complain of in Milton's *Lycidas*. *The Young Author* did not demonstrate that the young author was yet old enough for London.

Nor did *Irene*. *Irene* was a large, dismal, full-length tragedy, composed after Oxford but before London (it later played, and failed, in London), in which the lovely Greek maiden Irene held "in her chains the captivated Sultan" of Turkey, surrounded by an intolerable mix of Greeks and Turks, all sounding like bad English rhetoricians and talking abstractly of the evils of arbitrary power, and of evil itself:

> Did unresisted lightning aid their [the enemy's] cannon?
> Did roaring whirlwinds sweep us from the ramparts?
> 'Twas vice that shook our nerves, 'twas vice, Leontius,
> That froze our veins and wither'd all our powers.

Johnson must have hoped that the frozen veins of the Greeks would be taken as English veins too, but he was wrong to hope. The play never made it home. He had to go and live in London to learn the true home vices, and when he did he wrote the poem *London*, a much more direct and convincing outpouring than anything he had done before, and for my tastes superior to his later, more generalized *Vanity of Human Wishes*.

Before *London* the writing of verse had been an exclusively elevated undertaking for him, not of the earth he daily walked on. The city of London brought him down as a writer, made him see the possibility of literature with currency. London brought forth the side of him that would most benefit biography, and *London* was the first result. Its immediacy of shock and anger has not, I think, been sufficiently credited.

Krutch, for instance, blunts the anger in it by talking of how Johnson *enjoyed* being immersed in London's vice. And Wain diverts us by finding the poem's political anger typical of youth, and more lofty as anger than the scurrilous attack on Rome by Juvenal in his third satire, which the poem explicitly, and sometimes line-by-line, imitated. As for Bate, he says:

> But of course [*sic*] "London" was never really conceived as a "satire" —as a strongly impassioned sense of outrage (or indeed of an impassioned sense of anything else). Instead it was an exercise of talent, understandably designed to make an immediate appeal—to compensate for the failure of Irene, and make money for himself and even more for Tetty.

Despite Bate I must proclaim *London* satire, and intended as such, and impassioned satire at that (more on this below). It did serve Johnson practically, though, as his entry to Grub Street, and particularly to Edward Cave, a quiet, money-minded printer and editor of an important publication in the history of periodicals, the *Gentleman's Magazine*. Johnson submitted the poem to Cave under a pseudonym; Cave printed it and paid him £10 for it. The poem was a success, Johnson was revealed, Cave was pleased, and soon Johnson was working for him at a regular column of semifictional "Parliamentary Debates" that was to extract half a million words from him in the next few years. The "Debates" appeared at the time when Robert Walpole's long Whig leadership in Parliament was about to end, and gave Johnson sea-room politically, as well as practice in high rhetoric and irony. They are not relevant to this account, but their demands upon him certainly influenced his development, as did some quickie biographies he produced at about the same time of such figures as Sir Francis Drake. (The biographies were, Bate declares, largely translations, or cribbed from other biographies). These labors were businesslike hacking, and not written under his own name. Then came a quite different assignment, of his own devising, a life of the poet Richard Savage.

The Savage life, the first of Johnson's poet "lives," was unlike the others in emphasis. The others would be written thirty years later and be mostly about the poems of the poets. The Savage life was mostly about Savage. It was Johnson's last big effort for Cave. After it he began work on his immense dictionary, and undertook his own publications, the *Rambler* and the *Idler*. Also after it the road up for him became, in a sense, the road down, since Tetty died in 1752, his mother in 1759, and the rest of his life was devoted to stable, mature, long-term projects, including a long-delayed edition of Shakespeare and, finally, his *Lives of the Poets*. But *London* and the *Life of Savage* were both full of Johnson's energy, and neither was marked by his later self-satisfaction.

◆ ◆

First, *London*. Johnson was not a great poet, and his future after *London* was to be largely in prose, but in *London* he was quite at home and at ease, even though satire was new to him:

> Heroes, proceed! What bounds your pride shall hold?
> What check restrain your thirst for power and gold?
> Behold rebellious virtue quite o'erthrown,
> Behold our fame, our wealth, our lives your own.

These "heroes," unlike those in *Irene*, were not wandering about in Turkey. They were clearly located in England. They were local, venal politicians lusting after gold, and squeamish local laureates—he was thinking of Colley Cibber—blaming the decline of the nation not on greed but on "persecuting fate," in order to keep their pensions coming. Nor did the poem present the decline of a remote ancient culture, but London's own culture, where "all crimes [were] safe but hated poverty." The decline was eloquently, though ornately, asserted to be occurring in the here and now.

Modern critics' low opinion of the poem seems to be based in their wish to keep Johnson literarily aloft and out of politics. Bate is the most confusing here. He makes great capital of Johnson's several-year slavery to the "Parliamentary Debates," yet thinks those efforts were evidence not of political energy but merely of Johnson's role-playing as a Grub Street hack. I would say instead that Johnson's descent from Oxford's pastoral lyricism and tragedy into satire and political prose was a serious ideological move on his part toward what the city of London had at the time in the way of a counterculture.

That culture was largely Tory, but certainly not thereby rich. The

Whigs were the money people, and as Bate points out, they were the majority culture, the establishment culture. They were the ones under attack in *London*, which was of a piece politically with the Swift and Gay satires preceding it. Johnson himself must have thought of the poem as more than an exercise in imitation or he would not have filled it with such vigorous anger, and would not have had reason to submit it anonymously to Cave.

Both *London* and the "Parliamentary Debates" were, in other words, felt ventures, and the feelings Johnson expressed in them were much like those he brought to his *Life of Savage*. Savage was the self-proclaimed bastard son of the Countess of Macclesfield, and though writing of him was ostensibly just another journalistic opportunity (brought on by the sudden death of Savage in a debtor's prison), Johnson had *known* Savage and all the social-cultural ills churning around him. The closeness made the difference.

He had not known him long, but well enough to have, as Wain says, "prowled London's midnight streets" with him. Wain has been the biographer most touched by Johnson's affection, saying that "to the most unteachable, unredeemable Bohemian drifter he opened his heart in love, admiration and pity," and suggesting that Savage took the place of Tetty for him. (Tetty was drinking by then, and being "increasingly querulous.") Certainly Savage's financial and parental misfortunes were events Johnson could commune with, and he communed to the degree that he accepted Savage's tales without question. They were tales that modern scholarship has long been busy discrediting, but Johnson's naiveté was more than made up for by the intensity of his commitment. No later biography he undertook was at all like this one.

For the first few pages he lingered on the infamous conduct of Savage's supposed mother, saying that she had displayed "an implacable and restless cruelty." Then he moved to the infamous conduct of Savage's first patron, then to the infamous conduct of friends of Savage's who were involved in a barroom death for which Savage was blamed, and then to the conduct of a series of other patrons upon which he also passed judgment. The judgments were in Plutarch's tradition, but differed from Plutarch in that they were judgments of *private* conduct. They were judgments in which Johnson had a private interest. He had been living his subject's sorrows and angers, so he was delighted to think of Savage's patrons as "little creatures"—

Pope's phrase—and delighted with Savage's own description of their conduct as "perfidiousness improving upon perfidiousness, and inhumanity upon inhumanity." Savage was a cause.

But not a high literary cause. He was no Aristotelian hero, but a victimized common man on the unfriendly streets of life, "of middle stature, of a thin habit of body, a long visage, coarse features and melancholy aspect," who happened to be "in uncommon degree vigorous and active," and whose judgment was "eminently exact both with regard to writings and to men." His wisdom did not come from having studied with Athenian seers, but from his "knowledge of life," a knowledge derived from his illegitimacy and its social consequences. Savage, for Johnson, was a "natural" in the sense in which Edmund, in *King Lear*, was a natural. His origin placed him outside the customs and conditionings of society, giving him, for his time, special and novel biographical status.* He was not to be looked at primarily as a poet, or as a man of his age, or even as a victim of his age. He was, finally, only himself, "one soul moving between two definite events, birth and death."

And so Johnson was driven to focus on that soul to a degree that he was not by any other biographical subject. He brought in Savage's poetry only in passing, though admiring it: "His descriptions are striking, his images animated, his fictions justly imagined, and his allegories artfully purified; . . . his diction is elevated, though sometimes forced. . . . Of his style, the general fault is harshness, and its general excellence is dignity." Mainly he was interested in the man's character, not his writings, and he assessed the character with some defiance, finding Savage to be, despite his troubles, a man of "natural equity" and one "in favor of human nature." He applied the word *nature* to Savage in what was to be Rousseau's meaning for the term. Savage was a *good* Edmund, a *noble* Savage. His purities were not of the classical world of purity, or of the Christian world either, yet he was pure, a man "whose ideas of virtue might have enlightened the moralist, whose eloquence might have influenced senates, and whose

* In looking for illustrations for the first meaning of *nature* in his *Dictionary* ("an imaginary being supposed to preside over the material and animal world"), Johnson went to Edmund: "Thou, Nature, art my Goddess; to Thy Law my Services are bound." There were certainly more civilized views of nature in *King Lear* for him to have chosen, and in the play Edmund's various villainies are often even called *un*natural. There appears to have been a definite Edmund-Savage connection.

delicacy might have polished courts," if only the moralists, senates, and courts had agreed to listen.

• •

All grave spirits have been purifiers of sorts. There is little distinction in the process itself, since it can take so many forms. In modern times Marx, Freud, Hitler, vegetarians, environmentalists, feminists, and minimalists might be mentioned as purifiers—not a cohesive group. All they have in common is an urge to improve us, together with a faith that improvement is possible. But for the genre of biography Jean Jacques Rousseau as an improver was particularly important. A century before Freud he performed a function related to Freud's, in that his arguments for improving us by keeping us out of civilization's way separated the improving process from public, civilized duty, or service. Plutarch would have disliked him. Johnson made a show of detesting him. Boswell, a year after meeting Johnson, visited him "in a wild valley" and *liked* him. Later he asked Johnson if he thought Rousseau had been "bad company" for him, and Johnson replied: "Sir, if you are talking jestingly of this, I don't talk with you. If you mean to be serious, I think him one of the worst of men; a rascal who ought to be hunted out of society, as he has been." Johnson was explicitly annoyed by Rousseau's noble savage for trying to be primitive in a civilized age, and he gave Boswell a lecture about Rousseau's "running about town arguing the advantages of poverty" in a money world. Yet there was much of Rousseau in *Richard* Savage, though he was a city boy.

All this is to show that Johnson was predictably unpredictable. In language and in poetry, he sought the clear font but often praised the muddy waters of verbal "exuberance." In scholarship he was responsible and diligent (at least when young), but determinedly careless about being so, and ironic at the expense of "academic bowers." In literary criticism he was always to be found beating back the wilderness while confessing that he admired, was awed by, the wilderness. And in the world of London he walked about with a verbal club, assaulting such barbarians as the Americans, but at the same time searching out souls "in favor of human nature," with "natural equity," like Savage.

So all his life he rejoiced in Shakespeare as a natural genius who kept redeeming the natural for him. He thought Shakespeare a happy case of noble *im*purity. Let me recall his famous paragraph comparing

Shakespeare with correct and regular writers: "The work of a correct and regular writer is a garden accurately formed and diligently planted, varied with shades, and scented with flowers; the composition of Shakespeare is a forest, in which oaks extend their branches, and pines tower in the air, interspersed sometimes with weeds and brambles." Later in this paragraph Johnson shifted his metaphor and found Shakespeare opening up a mine full of gold and diamonds, though "debased by impurities." He could hardly praise the impurities outright, but he knew their presence was part of what he admired.

And he could also be attentive, guiltily attentive, to impurities in himself. I am suspicious of the prayers of Johnson that have been preserved—simply because they have been preserved—but they do show us a Christian conventionally but fervently penitent about his frailties, and pleading for personal purification. And with or without the prayers, we can surely say of him that he was not at all, in his own mind, a noble savage.

Out of these ambiguities came his more reflective, post-Cave writings, such as the short essays composing the Rambler and the Idler, essays with only occasional biographical focus. In his essay on biography in the Rambler (see appendix) he was strong on "observable particularities" and "personal knowledge," but in his writings of the time he did not follow his own instructions. He became instead the Great Moralist. He wrote 1,000-word pieces on "the folly of anger," "the causes of disagreement in marriage," "the importance of the early choice of a profession," "the requisites to true friendship," and on dozens of other abstract topics rendered lofty, and safe, by his balanced prose and wisdom. These writings brought him fame, and eventually a royal pension, putting him in line to be approached, befriended, and given a pundit role by Boswell; but they were not writings in which he often mentioned specific persons. And when he did so he described no live individuals like Savage, but created fictive, representative characters like Ned Drugget (Idler, no. 16), who became a successful tradesman and moved to the country, where he sat "at the window, counting the carriages as they passed before him"; or a mythical Ethiopian named Seged (Rambler, nos. 204 and 205), who, having solved all his state's problems, sought happiness. His most famous creation was the pompous, know-it-all critic Dick Minim (Idler, nos. 60 and 61), who sometimes sounded as officious as Johnson himself, but could be depended on to have ridiculous opinions unlike Johnson's. Of all these figures, Minim was obviously closest to home—bad critics were abounding—but even Minim was outside the province of biography. In creating them Johnson was partaking instead of the world of parable.

He did the same when he came to write *Rasselas, Prince of Abyssinia*, essentially an expansion of the *Rambler* essays on Seged. *Rasselas* was a quick move to pay urgent debts at the time of his mother's death. He wrote it evenings, in a week, and spoke of it later with scorn, though it did pay the debts. Wain describes it as a conventional "moral tale . . . a commonplace of Christian homiletics," in the tradition of "serious writers" of the time, but by "serious writers" he must have meant the writers of utopian fables, not biographies. To Johnson's credit the work emerged as something of a satire of that utopian tradition, roughly in the mode of *Gulliver's Travels*. It was less moral than morally escapist. It was utopian with an antiutopian drift. In it his unlikely prince, with the prince's unlikely sister, abandoned after a few pages the unlikely Eden valley of their birth and sought out something less boring. They wandered about the world trying everything, looking for the satisfaction of simply being satisfied. They did not find it. What, then, to do?

In any commonplace of Christian homiletics the satisfaction should then have been found in faith, but Johnson refused to reward the prince and his sister that way. He *left* them unsatisfied. Wain does not worry about the refusal, and Bate explains it away as Johnson's "inner taboo . . . against specific religious discussion in his writings." But I see in it a clear decision on Johnson's part against the pat formula, a bit of *black* sententiousness.

There should be no surprise here. He had much blackness in him. It was part of his intellectual strength, keeping him from being a Polonius. And at the time of *Rasselas* he was, he said himself, struggling so hard with his own "terrors and perplexities" that he nearly stopped writing. But the black ending to *Rasselas* did not remedy the paleness of the fable characters themselves. They were just talking heads. Johnson's prince, like Machiavelli's, existed only as a prop, and Johnson knew this, knew the thinness of the work, calling it "that little piece." Eighteen years passed before he came back to true biography, and by then he was aged, fixed in his anti-barbarian, Plutarchian ways. He could not then be black. His *Lives of the Poets*, appearing between 1779 and 1781, was full of high sentiments and broad views about mostly minor poets. In many ways it was the end point of classical biography.

◆ ◆

He had not been commissioned to write lives at all; he had been asked to write prefaces to an ambitious compilation of poets' works from the mid-seventeenth century to the near present (poets still alive were excluded). A consortium of booksellers had chosen him, thinking that he would write from two to five pages of biography for each poet, together with an "advertisement" for each. They imagined dozens of volumes, but those to which Johnson contributed finally numbered ten. In effect Johnson had marching orders to produce a mixture of biography and criticism for an anthology of fifty-two poets.

At the outset he referred to it as a minor event—"I am engaged to write Little Lives, and Little Prefaces, to a Little Edition of the English Poets"—and when a friend tried to help him search out authorities on the poets' backgrounds, he ridiculed her help, saying, "If it rained knowledge, I'd hold out my hand, but I would not give myself the trouble to go in quest of it." He was immensely well read, had an immense memory, knew where he was going, and was the great guru; so he escaped questing. Still, his handling of details was slapdash and superficial in comparison with the work of any serious modern biographer, and I would say it was slapdash in comparison with Plutarch too. Plutarch was thorough when he could be, and apologetic when he could not be. Johnson was not even apologetic. With facts that he scorned, such as those in the lives of poets that he scorned, he wasted no time at all. He would throw in a few facts from other biographers, acknowledge his debt to them, and push right past them to criticism and judgment of the poets' poems.

Boswell complained to him that he should not write about a poet the printers had chosen if he thought the poet was a dunce, but Johnson said he would do so "and *say* he was a dunce." He did say so, and sometimes he said so not about Pomfrets and Stepneys and Mallets and Fentons, but about poets not generally thought to be dunces, Thomas Gray for example. Gray was a popular, celebrated contemporary of Johnson's, and had died a few years before the writing of the *Lives*. Johnson supplied four pages of readily available information about his life, added an estimate of his character written by someone else, and then said: "Gray's poetry is now to be considered, and I hope not to be looked on as an enemy to his name if I contemplate it with less pleasure than his life." He then contemplated just one Gray poem with moderate pleasure, the *Elegy in a Country Churchyard*.

Behind his arrogant finality there was, especially with minor figures, much good sense. There was also his flair for pontifical comedy. (He keeps reminding me of W. C. Fields.) He was a wit who knew how effective a know-it-all rhetoric could be, and he pushed this pose endlessly. He will probably be chiefly remembered for his put-downs, such as "patriotism is the last refuge of a scoundrel" and "much may be made of a Scotchman if he be caught young"; and with bad poets he was in his element. The trouble was, there were too many bad poets, and thoroughly minor poets. He was awash in them. He did become seriously committed to describing with care a few poets of stature, but with the exception of those studies the project drove him to be critically godlike and biographically superficial. As a whole his *Lives* did not approach his own standards for biography, for which, he said, "a man must dive into the recesses of the human heart."

His inescapable trouble was with the quality of the poets, but he was also handicapped by the mechanical format he chose to work in, which did not encourage diving into recesses. He divided each life into three rough but usually distinct parts: (1) the subject's background and life; (2) the subject's character (that he was extravagant, profligate, sweet tempered, choleric, rich, poor, hypocritical, convivial); and (3) commentary on the subject's works, together with a final judgment. The early life produced the career, the career was amplified by description of the character, and the poems then remained to be described, one by laborious one, and assessment made. Sometimes he dealt with so many works that they occupied two-thirds of the whole, and his climactic summation of their worth made the "life" side of each essay merely prefatory and incidental. Yet the summations were not always meaty either. In them he leaned hard on the imprecise grandeur of musty adjectival value words such as "elegant-vulgar," "harsh-smooth," "bright-dark," and "noble-pretty." And, as always, his great forte was balanced syntactical phrasing that set the tone for punditry but was not always as revealing as it was meant to be. "[Edmund] Waller seems neither to have had a mind much elevated by nature, nor amplified by learning, . . . [yet] he added something to our elegance of diction, and something to our propriety of thought." Nicholas Rowe "seldom moves either pity or terror, but he often elevates the sentiments; he seldom pierces the breast, but he always delights the ear, and often improves the understanding." And John Sheffield "had the perspicuity and elegance of an historian, but not the fire and fancy of a poet."

Plutarch would have quickly recognized his own rhetorical procedures in Johnson's, but he might have complained about some of the fluff, and he certainly would have questioned the application of such solemnity to a few bales of couplets. Moreover, his questioning would have been just. The hand of God could not have been heavier than Johnson's as he descended on the fifty-two versifiers, but of the fifty-two, only a few seemed worth the attention. He might have done well to listen to his own satire of pompous Dick Minim, who could be depended upon to make much of little ("the greatest excellence," Minim once solemnly remarked, "is in the third line, which is crack'd in the middle to express a crack"). Johnson was himself too close to the poetic inflation of the time to be sensitive to it.

That inflation is hard to understand even now. Poets had always been in high places, but England in the seventeenth and eighteenth centuries had elevated them further, perhaps to replace the tarnished political leaders of the Protectorate, the Restoration, the "Glorious Revolution," and the endless Whig-Tory wars that Johnson grew up with. No Plutarch was anxious to "do" leaders like those, so that left the poets. They had become politicized and journalistic. They had influence. Johnson had lived with them, knew them, knew the absurdities intertwined with them, but in old age had ascended so high himself that the absurdities did not always strike home. Though the greatest generalist of his age, he gave no indication in the *Lives* of the generally infirm state of English poetry in 1780, no sign that the spirit of it, as seen in its brittle prosody and rationalist uses (Erasmus Darwin wrote a two-volume study of plant life *in couplets*), was dying. He was old. He was at his ease.

Even with the major poets he was, though detailed, superficial. He could not see the dim futures of Dryden and Addison, though he gave them many pages. His Plutarchian comparison of Dryden and Pope was so drily measured that Bate diagramed it to show Johnson's syntactical balancings:

Of genius
    that power which constitutes a poet
    that power without which
        judgement is cold
        and
        knowledge is inert;
    that energy which collects, combines,
        amplifies and animates;

the superiority must, with some hesitation,
    be allowed to Dryden.

Perhaps, though, in the demotion of Pope, he did show a bit of pre-
science. He admired Pope, but from a distance. He knew that Pope's
genius, which he acknowledged, had been limited by prosodic preci-
osity, and he put him down firmly at several points. He regretted, for
instance, that following the early "Essay on Criticism," Pope was
"ever after at a stand," and he said of the later "Essay on Man,"
"Never were penury of knowledge and vulgarity of sentiment so
happily disguised." He was too much of a classicist to be ready for the
Nietzsches and Kierkegaards ahead, but he was not always at home,
though a classicist, with the status quo either.

It was therefore with the unruly figures, Milton and Swift, that he
could extend himself, as he had with Savage thirty years earlier. He
could treat them as if they were the enemy—Milton especially—but
he could admire them too. They were great talents in his own contrar-
ious mode.

He professed to *despise* Milton, so his friends "trembled" when he
sat down to do Milton's life. Milton, he said, was all stubbornness,
rebelliousness, and plain "savageness"—common features, he
thought, of Puritans. Milton was a man of changeable convictions,
unhealthy educational notions, crude invective, dubious faith in the
Almighty, and of course absolutely licentious theories of government. His republicanism encompassed nearly everything that threat-
ened the stability of mankind. It was

> founded in an envious hatred of greatness, and a sullen desire of in-
> dependence; in petulance impatient of control, and pride disdainful
> of superiority. He hated monarchs in the state, and prelates in the
> church; for he hated all whom he was required to obey. It is to be
> suspected, that his predominant desire was to destroy rather than
> establish, and that he felt not so much the love of liberty as repug-
> nance to authority.

In other words Milton was his own Satan, just as—in a strange,
underground way—Johnson himself was. Johnson could not bring
himself to like *Paradise Lost*—its perusal was "a duty rather than a
pleasure"—but he paid it and its author homage anyway by the fury
of his attack, and by concluding with qualified high praise as if he had
not already wiped him off the face of the earth:

From his contemporaries he neither courted nor received support; there is in his writings nothing by which the pride of other authors might be gratified, or favour gained, no exchange of praise, nor solicitation of support. His great works were performed under discountenance, and in blindness; but difficulties vanished at his touch; he was born for whatever is arduous; and his work is not the greatest of heroic poems, only because it is not the first.

In much of this passage Johnson could well have been describing his own best features: great independence, high principles, and high aims. With Milton he was not placid and comfortable, any more than he was with himself. He raged at the man, while at the same time communing with him.

As a Tory, Swift had a big initial advantage over Milton, but Johnson began by being equally suspicious of his character. He thought Swift was not manfully open in defending himself, describing him as one who shuffled between "cowardice and veracity." He thought him "too fond of singularity," and "desirous to make a mode of happiness for himself different from the general course of things, and order of Providence." And he could only with the "greatest difficulty . . . discover by what depravity of intellect [Swift] took ideas from which every other mind shrinks with disgust." In other words Swift, unlike Savage, was not "in favor of human nature." The genius in him had not performed morally in creating the Yahoos.

As for Swift's poetry, it was "what the author intended . . . humorous, almost always light." The diction was "correct," the numbers "smooth," and the rhymes "exact." The poetry occupied Johnson for one short paragraph, and *Gulliver's Travels* took not much longer. Swift should not have been a light poet, but he should not have been a prose satirist either. Somewhere, somehow, he should have aimed at sublimity, but did not. He was a misanthrope whose imagination dwelt on "disease, deformity and filth," who "relieved without pity, and assisted without kindness; so that those who were fed by him could hardly love him." Yet (with Johnson there is always a *yet*) he "for a time dictated the political opinions of the English nation," and "it was from the time when he first began to patronize the Irish that they may date their riches and prosperity." Johnson then ended with the following praise, more cautious than that for Milton, but also directed at the special, nonconformist character of Swift's genius: "Perhaps no writer can easily be found that has borrowed so little, or that in all his excellences and all his defects has so well maintained his claim to be an original.

◆ ◆

In his *Dictionary*'s first definition of *genius* Johnson interestingly muddled the civilized and innate senses of the word. The definition itself was traditional—"the protecting or ruling power of men, places and things"—but the two examples of the word's usage, both from Shakespeare, were slightly off the sense of the definition:

> —There is none but he
> Whose being I do fear; and, under him,
> My genius is rebuk'd; as it is said
> Antony's was by Caesar.
> > —*Macbeth* 3.1

> The genius and the mortal instruments
> Are then in council,
> And the state of man, like to a little kingdom,
> Suffers insurrection.
> > —*Julius Caesar* 2.1

In their original contexts each speech was spoken by a person whose genius seemed to be native to him, and who was up against the king or the "protecting or ruling" genius to which the definition itself refers. In the quotation from *Macbeth* Banquo was the legitimate ruler whose power Macbeth's unanointed genius had to fear. In the quotation from *Julius Caesar* the speaker was Brutus, also a rebel, and himself the "state" suffering insurrection. Surely the *classical* sense of genius was poorly illustrated by giving genius over to rebels, no matter how just their cause. Yet Shakespeare did it. And Johnson, that ferocious critic of rebellion against authority, followed suit.

I cannot make a rebel of him from two quotations, any more than I can cancel the antiquarian classicism dominant in most of his "lives," but I do think that the quotations show his attraction, which was lifelong, to the "shadow"* side of human nature, which Shake-

---

* I am thinking of the word as used by Jung, who simply describes it as the side of our personality we repress. Unlike Freud, his approach to it is social. Thus he says that Western man collectively sees "the face of his own evil shadow" grinning at him from the other side of the iron curtain. Jung's approach seems more readily applicable to Johnson than Freud's, but Bate refers only to Freud.

speare also was fascinated by, in Brutus, Macbeth, Hamlet, Angelo, and others. Johnson was attracted to it but frightened by it, and modern scholars have made much of his fears, presenting evidence like the padlock he bought to lock himself up with, should he feel he needed to be restrained, and the hysterical moment reported by his friend Mrs. Thrale when he fell to his knees before a minister and prayed to God "to continue to him the uses of his understanding." The writing disciplines that he imposed upon himself kept him from such injurious depressions except, apparently, during two periods of his life— one at Oxford, and one in London when he was in his mid-fifties— but the depressive streak in him did not go away. My sense of him is that he constantly thought of taking his own life, and constantly told himself not to. He knew himself well, and Bate has made much of his knowledge of human depths, saying that he was imbued with Freud's "reality principle," but Bate has neglected, I think, the compensatory process in Johnson of denying what he knew. The compensating made him the moralist, classicist, royalist, and rationalist that he was.

He is praised for having refuted Berkeley's argument against the existence of matter by kicking a rock, but I suggest that all his life he tried to refute the *rock* by ignoring it. In a way he made his whole career out of refuting the rock.

Thus we would not have had the *Lives of the Poets* if he had not told himself he had a gathering of poets of some worth on his hands, though he knew (so Boswell reported) that the project was largely designed for "the promotion of piety." He provided many honesties as he went along, but he would have been much more honest with himself if he had cut out half the poets and faced up cleanly to why he found Milton and Swift more exciting than Dryden and Pope.

The immense anthology, of which his poets were only a part, came to over sixty volumes, and was an establishment project to the roots, a Williamsburg project, a restoration project with no overseeing intelligence of his stature. Its emptiness was shown by what happened to it after publication. It quickly died, and his *Lives* were excerpted from it so that literary criticism could proceed all by itself.

The *Lives of the Poets* was his most popular work in the first half of the nineteenth century, but not because of his handling of Milton and Swift. Rather, his apologists felt steadily obliged to gloss over his damnations and to emphasize his "balance." The *Lives* lived on not because it was provocative but because Johnson was seen by nineteenth-century conservatives as the last moralist and traditionalist they could rely on in an age that had abandoned the rational to indiscriminate self-indulgence.

In other words he was respected for the image he had managed to project of himself—much aided by Boswell—in his great guru days. His admirers ignored the side of him that was *not* like that.

And with regard to the *Lives* the admirers were generally right. The *Lives* was an extended classical exercise in subordinating the self to the accomplishments it left for posterity. Of Johnson's fifty-two poets, the *characters* of only six or seven—including Savage, Milton, and Swift—were even mentioned in his final summations. His underlying assumption about character was clear in the last paragraph of his life of Prior, where he made Prior's conduct on public occasions the source also of his best poetry:

> In his private relaxation he revived [in his verse] the tavern, and in his amorous pedantry he exhibited [in his verse] the college. But on higher occasions, and nobler subjects, when habit was overpowered by the necessity of reflection, he wanted not wisdom as a statesman, or elegance as a poet.

The inclination now, I think, would be to turn the key terms of that statement around, making the verses reveal that Prior had in him the qualities of a statesman but was also serious-minded. Then the biographer would tell us *why* Prior was so serious on state occasions, and at other times not, doubtless revealing that Prior had creatively opposed psychic obligations within himself!

One of the memorable remarks of E. E. Cummings, made in a "non-lecture" at Harvard, was that he had yet to meet (he was then about sixty) "a single peripherally located ego." The remark is, I would say, on the order of a great truth, so I do not wish to detract from it when I say that it is also in a sense false. It is false even about Cummings, who was as egotistical as most poets. It is false because each of the poems of Cummings, though a manifestation of Cummings's ego, has gone out from him and is now peripherally located in any reader's head.

Poems go out from their poets and come to represent them while also abandoning them, just as Lycurgus's laws went forth from Lycurgus, but also passed beyond him. Between the accomplishments of an ancient Greek or Roman and the accomplishments of a Cummings, there is a vital connection, and the connection is vital for biography. Ancient biographers—that is, biographers right up to the time of Johnson—thought the accomplishments of statesmen or poets were, in effect, displaced egos, and the displacement was thought wholly proper, moral, purificatory. The displacement was not a masking of the "true" self, but rather a normal, healthy action of the self. Johnson inherited that public imperative in the self's make-up, believed in it except in shadow moments, and was largely led by it in the *Lives*.

The *Lives*, then, is essentially bound up in the old dispensation about selves, though, as I have indicated, the most energetic moments in it occurred when Johnson became dissatisfied with the displacement and began dealing with an ego directly. In those moments he was awed by ego—the bigger the better—and shifted his focus to it. The *Lives* is therefore a strange mixture.

Modern criticism oddly retains a good deal of this mixing in what we now call "critical biography"—that is, the biographies of writers, musicians, and artists which are at the same time critical assessments. Bate—I think rightly—attributes the features of critical biography in part to Johnson, though he does not emphasize, as I have been doing, its indeterminacy. To me it seems that Johnson stands not only at the end of an age of biography but also at the beginning of a new age, one that still does not know what it wants from the genre.

VI

—And the Boswell Connection

Ten years after their first meeting Johnson and Boswell toured the Hebrides together. Upon their return Johnson wrote, in twenty days, an extended account of the trip, which was published in 1775. Then, a year after Johnson's death, Boswell published his own journal of the trip, 300 pages that were really a section of his Johnson biography. (He sent them forth, W. Jackson Bate reports, as a "trial balloon" a year before the biography itself.) The difference between the two reports is that Johnson was interested in the Hebrides, and Boswell was interested in Johnson. Krutch declares that Johnson is more interesting than the Hebrides, which may be so, but he fails to mention—and neither does Wain or Bate—that Boswell's interest in Johnson was not just the interest of a simple, burrowing biographer. He was interested in Johnson's Scotland appearance in the way a circus promoter is interested in a sword-swallower or a fat lady. He was putting Johnson on exhibit. Johnson was much more considerate of the Hebrides. He was studying them.

It is true that any biography has something of the character of an exhibit, but in this instance Boswell was being unusually promotive. He was showing off his catch to his own countrymen—and then writing up their responses—in a way that made the performance both public and stagey. Such a manner is not characteristic even of modern biographies, except the popular ones about "superstars"; but Boswell knew he had an eighteenth-century superstar. And he certainly had promoter instincts. And he was at home.

I wish I could say that Johnson did not know he was being made a sideshow, but according to Boswell, Johnson read Boswell's journal regularly on their trip, and approved it. In Boswell's hands Johnson became, even before his arrival in Scotland, a "valuable acquisition" (as Boswell put it to a prospective Scottish host), one whom Boswell advertised as a "mighty sage," eliciting red-carpet treatment everywhere they went. Biography of the inner man does not thrive on display, except inferentially, yet much of Boswell's approach to biography was built on it. When the two men arrived in the civilized parts of Scotland, Boswell led his sage before all the appropriate dignitaries, and set him down to discourse with them upon any subject that was floated his way. The dignitaries expected him to be witty at the expense of Scotland, and he was. The dignitaries asked him to make judgments on many matters—such as law, emigration, wealth, poverty, "ouran-outangs" and David Hume—and he did. He proved himself able to be instantly definitive about anything at all, and to be so in balanced phrases too. Thus, of dueling and of law: "As it was found that in a duel, he who was in the right had not a better chance than he who was in the wrong, therefore society instituted the present mode of trial, and gave the advantage to him who was in the right."

In other words, like any good performer, Johnson rose to the performance asked of him, and having been tested by the learned, allowed himself to be carried off to the wilds. There he was put on show as an aging urbanite determined to rough it, and he performed well in that role too. Mostly. He refused to be discomposed by several wild rides in small craft on the open Atlantic. He fell from a horse but calmly "got up immediately." He stoically put up with the infinitely bad weather, except at one point late in the trip when he said: "I want to be on the mainland, and go on with existence. This is a waste of life." He even composed an ode to the Isle of Skye (in Latin), and in all the inns and castles where he was entertained he kept talking, talking. It must have been great sport for Scotland to hear him talking. His was a good show.

But it was a show, and as a show it had some of the qualities of vaudeville. As reported by Boswell, it was a miscellany, a series of unrelated, though mostly intellectual, acts. Johnson discoursed on all subjects, hence on no subject, not being on display to discourse on any subject. He was on display to show how a mighty discourser did what he did.

In contrast, Johnson's account of the trip was a well-ordered travelogue. Though as heavily weighted with his opinions as Boswell's journal had been with his, it had, in the fashion of the day, a clear social mission. Johnson was studying the natives and their culture. He did so. He clambered around in a desolate spot, examined a ruin, and reported that it had been brought to its state "by the intestinal tumult of the barbarous ages." After climbing a small mountain, he noted that "mountainous countries contain the original, or at least the oldest, race of inhabitants," because they have been able to expose assailants to "every power of mischief." He became minutely attentive to the culture of the natives and to their language. And as always he found uses for the minutiae by drawing generalizations from them about the culture. Krutch is quite right that what he reported about the culture is now less interesting than Johnson himself, but my point here is that Boswell's report on him was unfocused, miscellaneous, and (as Krutch himself points out) gossipy, while Johnson's report was clear, incisive, and directed away from gossip. He had plenty of opinions, but he put them in context, made them locally applicable.

Here, I think, is a great dividing point in the history of biography. Boswell in his Hebrides journal—and then in his opus on Johnson—shifted the subject of biography decisively over to a character as himself, and after Boswell the genre rapidly accommodated itself to the shift. Now, whether a subject is a king or an oil tycoon, a biographer is not encouraged to move from king to kingship, or from tycoon to dependence on the tycoon's fuel. He is to think of any such movement as diversionary, a part of the "broad views" approach that Edmund Gosse warned biographers against. Not only had Johnson never received any such warning, but if he had, he would have said that the warner was a blockhead. (He liked that word.) And he was as clearly directed toward broad views in his *Lives of the Poets* as he was in his handling of the Hebrides tour.

As I hope I have made clear, Johnson's approach was thoroughly Aristotelian. Character was not the main show. "The plot," said Aristotle, "is the first principle, and, as it were, the soul of a tragedy. Character holds the second place." And character held second place for Plutarch. And it held second place with the hagiographers as well, and with Vasari, Holinshed, and the rest. It held second place for Johnson too. He customarily subordinated character to the surround of character, just as he subordinated tulip stripes to tulips. Accepting the subordination principle did not mean that he had no interest in character, or lacked perception about it. It meant that when his orderly mind settled down to compose a biography, it let that principle order the work.

Bate writes at length about the principle of "protective subordination" in Johnson, pointing to it as the source of Johnson's lifelong approval of governmental order and regulation (to protect the vulnerable) and of his annoyance with the Whigs and with laissez faire—that is, with *un*subordinated mercantilism. But Bate will not apply the principle to Johnson's practice of biography. There he sees Johnson committed to exploring the unsubordinated individual in his "total experience." He seems to be thinking of the Savage life primarily, but the Savage life is unrepresentative. In biography as well as politics and business Johnson was a lifelong subordinator of individual selves.

The importance of the subordination principle for Johnson carries over to his rooted unlikeness to Boswell. As all the biographers report, Johnson was a disciplined writer who, while flailing himself for laziness, was not lazy at all. He was always capable of putting out, and he did put out. He would have been a great Spartan under Lycurgus, and though his discipline may be explained away either by his need to combat his physical infirmities or by his simple need for money, there it was, part of him.

Boswell must have had discipline hidden away in his make-up too, or he would not have been able to keep his immense journals; but the evidence of his lack of discipline is much more impressive. As even his defenders point out, he was a rioteur who haunteden folye. One of them, Claude Colleer Abbott—whose lecture on the searches for Boswell's papers is marvelously brief—sums him up well:

> There is the disreputable Boswell of low life who sallies forth into London streets "like a roaring Lion after girls." There is the man who pleads with Temple, "Can I do better that keep a dear infidel for my hours of Paphian bliss?"—While at the same time he pursues, for the purposes of marriage, a covey of heiresses.

And the most cogent biographical piece I have read about him is called *Boswell's Clap*, by a literary pathologist, Dr. William B. Ober. For forty pages Ober traces, with a chronological chart, Boswell's nineteen attacks of urethritis between 1760 and 1790. The attacks were brought on by contacts with prostitutes that Boswell himself dutifully recorded. Ober draws no moral, but does make a case that Boswell's "exuberance" was excessive.

So friend and doctor alike agree that Boswell was not pure. My point is that the impurity, or exuberance, carried over into his work as a biographer, and while not perhaps describable there as a vice, has surely been overrated as a virtue. In biography Boswell was an easy, fluent writer with little interest in ordering, directing, editing his material. Of the 1,400 pages of his Johnson opus (not including the Hebrides trip), 1,100 pages are essentially journal entries—that is, records of his meetings with Johnson, plus their correspondence when they were separated. Between 1763 and 1784 they met perhaps three hundred times. The dates of the meetings are part of the data provided, as are the names of persons who joined them, and comments on their credentials and characters. If a meeting occurred in a tavern, the tavern would be named, and if the tavern proved to be a good one, and Johnson in good humor, Johnson would say a few sage words about taverns ("No, sir; there is nothing that has yet been contrived by man, by which so much happiness is produced as by a good tavern or inn"). If they happened to go to church together, and then walked back to Johnson's establishment, Johnson might censure "the licensed stews at Rome" and make comments about the need for "severe laws, steadily enforced . . . against those evils," since "all men will naturally commit fornication, as all men will naturally steal." If they were to dine with a certain Dr. Butter ("whose lady is daughter of my cousin, Sir John Douglas, whose grandson is now presumptive heir of the noble family of Queensbury"), Johnson might launch into a discourse on medicine, and then be led off into any number of other subjects. If any order appeared in the sequence, it was apt to be supplied by Johnson. The randomness was Boswell's largely. It was built into his way of life and thought, and into his way of biography.

His biography of Johnson has been praised for so long and so widely for its randomness, its *impurity*, and the resultant breadth of wisdom and character-probing it displays, that I cannot resist raising objections (though I will return to the praise). First, while giving great-talker Johnson the chance to talk greatly about all things, it also gave him a chance to be a bore. A reader can pick up the biography at any point, and put it down at any point, and be as well read in it (so long as a sizable chunk is read) as someone who proceeds dutifully through it from page one. In fact, to be dutiful is to be lulled to sleep by the awareness that what is happening is a continuum going nowhere. The volume's index—not its author or subject—gives it order and direction.

And second, the randomness of the biography is not as random as it seems to be, or as its backers make out. The backers say that in putting everything down Boswell avoided being tendentious, avoided the mistakes of classical biography committed by Johnson himself. But a randomness in parlor or tavern, under the conditions promoted by Boswell and recognized by Johnson, is really quite contrived. Even in our own indecorous time, and even under conditions of presumed privacy and frankness, such as an analyst's office, a person aware of what a listener seems to want can improvise many facts and roles to please him. Johnson knew what Boswell wanted—high polemic, balanced outrage, clever wisdom. He provided. The biographical art that Boswell passed on was that of the extended interview, and the limits of the interview as biography are that it is by nature a public event. The interviewed one says what he knows will be reported. He may or may not say what he thinks. Modern, whole biography, reaching for the heart's recesses, tries to deal with what the subject thinks as well, and in doing so has to range beyond the statements in an interview, as in my opinion Boswell was not disposed to do. He was not a prober, not an analyst, not a critic.

He was not even disposed to look critically at Johnson's literary works. With them he was merely an encomiast. Thus he declared the poem *London* to "have burst forth with splendor the rays of which will ever encircle his name." For him the works were simply further miscellaneous splendors from the mind of the great genius he was leading through the world, and he was not inclined to order the splendors except as any promoter or journalist orders material. Modern critical biography at its best does have, despite its confusions, the controlling agency of the critic's mind at work, as Johnson's assessing mind was at work in his *Lives of the Poets*. The modern biographies I have been referring to here—by Krutch, Wain, and Bate—are of this order, and though I have been arguing steadily with Bate, I think his biography is a fine example of the ordering impulse in biography. It is full, but not randomly, exhaustively inclusive. It is channeled to give us a whole Johnson, a Johnson beyond the public Johnson.

Boswell's mind did not lead him that way, and his basic approach is well illustrated in his early interviews of Rousseau in the wild valley. Over a period of two or three weeks he met several times with Rousseau in Rousseau's home, usually in the presence of a housekeeper, and he badgered the man to speak of great subjects in the way that Boswell wanted him to speak of great subjects. Later on Boswell would brag of his talents as a strategist in setting up and directing conversations, but what he managed to do with Rousseau was to shut him, slowly, up. Rousseau was an old, angry man and began their tête-à-tête by observing that "the French were a contemptible nation." Soon he was saying (still of the French), "Mankind disgusts me." But then Boswell went about his strategizing, trying to persuade Rousseau to talk about the Spanish, about the Scotch, about Boswell! Unfortunately Rousseau was soon saying less and less, Boswell more and more, and by the third or fourth interview Boswell decided—and told him he had decided—that Rousseau was "simple": "I expected to find you quite different to this: the great Rousseau. But you do not see yourself in the same light as others see you." The fact is that Boswell had not allowed Rousseau to present himself as Rousseau had planned to present himself. Rousseau was obviously not a person who was ready, like Johnson, to discourse about any topic. He needed to carry the ball himself to carry it well. Boswell wanted him to be the great Rousseau on Boswell's terms, and when Rousseau did not meet the terms, Boswell found him to be simple.

Yet Boswell came away thinking, "I shall be upheld forever by the thought that I am linked to M. Rousseau."

Unlike Rousseau, Johnson responded positively to Boswell's treatment, but in both cases the administrator of the treatment was so full of his own promotional designs that he was not really listening to the cases. I do not know Boswell's private history well enough—except through intermediaries like Dr. Ober—to know what it was that he was listening to, but it was in Scotland, not London or the wild valley.

In any case, I question the value of heavy strategizing in such instances. It goes against the principle of randomness for which Boswell is praised. Yet this strategizing produced one of the great biographies of all time, a milestone in the maturing of biography. The merits of the work are indisputable. Never before had so much material been amassed in the way of actual conversation with a great mind. Never had there been a loyal disciple so industrious in walking about with pen and paper and dutifully collecting his subject's pearls. And, therefore, never before had wholeness in biography been so strenuously reached for.

The best evidence of the magnitude of Boswell's contribution to the genre is the magnitude of the scholarly operations about him in recent decades, particularly at Yale. Yale obtained a castleful of his papers in the 1930s (the procuring was a long adventure tale, beginning in 1925), and since then the edited results have been appearing regularly, with, I believe, eighteen volumes now in print of Boswell's journals (found in the castle), plus later additions (from several Scottish attics). The whole of modern biographical scholarship totters if the merit of what Boswell squirreled away is not acknowledged. I feel very lucky that he is not my subject here.

My subject is not Boswell for the simple reason that Boswell has been made too much of in the history of biography. His contributions to the genre were great, yet there was a genre of biography before he arrived, and there were non-Boswellian forms of the genre after he departed. Pre-Boswellian biography, based on the ancient principles of Plutarch and Johnson, can still be seen at work in modern "critical" biography, and, though deviously, in some political biographies. It can even be seen, again deviously, in psychobiography, where the effort has been to find a psychic center to the biographee—that is, a dominant ordering force in a person's life. Boswell's impulses were not toward a center, but were endlessly centrifugal, pushing outward to miscellaneous exhibits. Some of his influence upon modern biography has therefore been successfully combatted, thank heaven. Printing the complete contents of a journal-diary or a castle is not the only, and may not be the best, way to come at knowledge of selves.

VII

Laurence Sterne: An Eighteenth-Century Wild Card

In these essays on early biography I have described the ancient convention of putting together groups of lives, the groupings being determined by social rank and function, or by profession. I started with Plutarch's *Lives of the Noble Grecians and Romans*, and worked through lives of saints, artists, and kings to Samuel Johnson's *Lives of the Poets*, noting that the center for these enterprises was not the self—though the self kept asserting its presence—but the character and standards of each group.

I have also described, in passing, some of the apparent origins of single-self lives not tied to groups, origins that seem to have been mostly outside biography, in memoirs, autobiography, and wholly separate genres. Arriving at last in the eighteenth century, in England, I have posited Johnson and Boswell as transitional figures, entertaining both group and self standards for the genre; and I would be happy to stop with Johnson and Boswell if I did not think it unscholarly to suggest that the transition from ancient to modern standards in the genre was simple. There is nothing simple about the history of biography, so I must be conscientious and end by introducing confusion.

The confusion began on the Continent, as I did try to show while passing swiftly through the Renaissance. It began in the novel, in comedy, and even in political writings such as Machiavelli's *Prince*. It began in all the literary forms that gave authors a chance to break rules and be *uncustomary*, as early biography did not. By the seventeenth and eighteenth centuries most of the genres were full of such opportunity, especially in England.

Perhaps the eccentrics were responsible. England's population of eccentrics has been one of that island's great resources since the beginnings of its assertion of a national identity, and the ranks of eccentrics swelled greatly after Elizabeth. They sat in their cold, stone chambers spilling hot, Raleighian ashes on their tweeds, and becoming, inadvertently, the backbone of English creativity and scholarship. Within biography itself a fine early example was seventeenth-century John Aubrey's *Brief Lives*. Aubrey was an antiquary "devoid of literary talent"* who studied ancient monuments, was constantly in law suits, lost his whole inheritance, and produced a large collection of oddly specific brevities—call them curiosities—about odd people, mostly his friends. Then, as a good seventeenth-century instance of a single life, there was Izaak Walton's tribute to John Donne, whose sermons in St. Paul's stirred Walton as a young man. Walton also wrote four other biographies, of fifty to eighty pages, on persons within his own world of loyal churchmen and royalists. The works were all commemorative and all well researched, but today they ring eccentrically to a modern ear because they are so heavy on rhetorical tropes and sonorities. The Donne life in particular has the sound of a speech by a tedious nobleman in one of Shakespeare's histories, with extended editorial platitudinizing on love ("a passion that carries us to commit errors with as much ease as whirlwinds move feathers"), wealth (it "hath seldom been the portion and never the mark to discover good people"), and the good old days ("when the clergy were looked upon with reverence and deserved it").

Neither Aubrey nor Walton had serious worries about what was customary in biography—except that Walton assumed that his role was to praise—and their individualism helped make the genre fluid. But more important help came later, from now-celebrated figures in the worlds of private journals and fiction. Let me take just three classics from the pre-Boswellian period—all odd in the best English way—as brief evidence of the favorable cultural climate for expanding biography's base: Pepys' *Diary*, Defoe's *Moll Flanders*, and, above all, Sterne's *Tristram Shandy*.

◆ ◆

Though English, I have never felt the attraction of Pepys' diary. My private complaint is that it goes on and on. Pepys wanders into

*Richard Garnett, in *Dictionary of National Biography*, s.v. "Aubrey, John."

town each weekday to talk with a commissioner, or an alderman, or a mighty lord, has a velvet coat made, carries funds or writs or gold plate to someone in the navy, has a lunch of lobster and wine, and talks "like a fool till four o'clock." Then he goes home and finds that his wife "has a mind to some cabbage" or perhaps "a calf's head carboned," but that she has just tried on her new petticoat and left her clothes strewn about, so they argue.

On sabbaths or special days he listens to a dull sermon, or perhaps runs over to Charing Cross to see a major-general hanged, drawn, and quartered, then returns to his wife to find her clothes strewn about, and to argue with her about keeping the dog, or the monkey, in the cellar, while perhaps entertaining a friend with claret, along with "botargo and butter and bread till twelve at night . . . and so to bed, very near fuddled." Meanwhile history is being made by the Restoration or the Plague, guns are being fired off, corpses dragged away in the night, and down at the bottom of each page, courtesy of modern scholarship, footnotes of a most particular kind are flowing, identifying a cast of characters now infinitely obscure. The cumulative effect is an amazingly British piece of reportage with amazing juxtapositions, artless ironies, and sophisticated chaos. There is no visible ordering at all, other than day-by-day chronology. There is also no probing of the past, or the inner life, or the meaning of things, no generalizing beyond the simplicities of good and bad, drunk and sober. As a demonstration of steady, experiential, domestic truth-telling, it has, I think, no equal, and both history and biography must be ever beholden to it for what it is. Yet it does, as I say, go on and on. Somehow my temperament reacts to it as Pepys reacted to his wife's strewn clothes.

As for *Moll Flanders*, it is, being fiction, far more pointed. In it, as in *Robinson Crusoe* and *Colonel Jack*, Defoe chose to describe a wholly private life, with its historically inconsequential details, while speeding up the Pepys reportorial procedure and being, quietly, orderly. Is not a genre an ordering? Defoe thought so. He was not a diarist or an historian, but a novelist—though a novelist before novelists knew what novels were supposed to be—and as a novelist he excised great quantities of matter that would have appeared in Moll's diary, had she begotten one. Also as a novelist, he chose for a heroine someone who, unlike Pepys, was not serving her country or company or patron, and was not even serving her own spiritual welfare until about page 300. Until page 300 she was a moral outcast, though largely by chance, and guilty of all the crimes Defoe could think of, starting with "open avowed incest and whoredom." She was also one of the world's millions of conspicuously unimportant subjects for a "life," such as, in our time, Willie Loman. How did Defoe render her important?

For one thing he played the role of moralist, and so aimed at displaying, as he said in his introduction, "a wicked life repented of." After page 300 he had Moll triumph over her Newgate past, and with renewed purity settle on a lovely plantation on the York River in Virginia, "with the stock of servants and cattle upon it," and a considerable fortune in worldly goods arriving by the boatload from England. Thus did he impose the form of a popular sentimental genre upon her.

But his moralist stance in the genre is now less interesting than his extensive social reporting as he went along. He was a good early sociologist, and in Moll Flanders he undertook to describe the plight of the debtor, the prisoner, the underprivileged self generally, but especially the plight of woman. He took on his female persona with verve, and came to sound—at least to this male reader—like an angry eighteenth-century feminist, especially as he described male dominance of the marriage market. In doing so he also, incidentally, explored the possibilities of autobiography as a manipulatable form, and directed it to serve his own purposes.

One of these purposes was to say, of Moll, what Arthur Miller said later about Willie Loman, that uncelebrated and flawed humans have to be respected too. The complete title of Moll Flanders was The Fortunes and Misfortunes of the Famous Moll Flanders, and Defoe meant by famous more than infamous. Underlying his account was a democratic theme: a self is a self is a self, to be communed with and written about—as Johnson himself, not much later, proposed in his essay on biography (see appendix).

As for Tristram Shandy, it is of course the finest book ever written, and being so has naturally attracted many enthusiasts. One of them, a friend of mine,* long ago wrote a doctoral thesis about its effect on other works, and managed to show that it significantly influenced not only all the literature that came after it but also most of the literature that came before.

There is, it is true, an opposing school of thought—in literary circles there always is—declaring that Sterne, far from being a great

---

*Professor Wayne Booth, who wrote his thesis on Sterne.

influence, was greatly influenced, in fact influenced by practically
everyone who picked up a pen, but particularly Lucian, Cervantes,
Rabelais, Swift, and Arbuthnot. And particularly also Shakespeare
and John Locke. And *most* particularly Robert Burton in *The Anatomy
of Melancholy*. Furthermore, says the opposing school, Sterne was an
exhibitionist, a poseur, and a money grubber, and when the first two
books of *Tristram Shandy* made him suddenly a celebrity (at that time
Voltaire called him the English Rabelais), and made *Shandyism* a literary household word, he lost most of the dubious integrity he had,
with the result that the later parts of *Tristram Shandy*, as well as the
work that followed it, *A Sentimental Journey*, became largely hackwork
written for large advances. Johnson was of this opposing school, did
not talk much about Sterne's works, but referred to him slightingly,
and once acknowledged that he had read some of Sterne's sermons
but only when he was stuck in a coach for an hour or so with no other
reading matter.

And then there was Oliver Goldsmith, who summed up the strict
moralist view by calling *Tristram Shandy* mere "bawdy and pertness,"
of a kind that could be produced by the "merest blockhead."

To appease both schools I here announce that both are partly
right, but I will refer mostly to the pro-Sterne school, especially to a
now-ancient Sterne biography by a Sterne enthusiast, Professor Wilbur Cross. Cross well illuminated Sterne's literary development, even
though he was very decorous about Sterne's sexuality, and a bit patronizing about the crudeness of Sterne's psychology. His biography
still seems to be the most complete single biographical source we
have, and all that a nonspecialist needs to adjudicate between the opposing schools, except a volume of letters, and of course Sterne's
works themselves.

Sterne was a wit from the start, though not a Shandean wit until
age forty-five, the year he wrote, in about six months, the first two
books of *Tristram Shandy*. He was a child of a needy branch of a respectable Church of England family. His father, married to an "ill-
bred" Irish woman, was a military man always in motion from one
station to another. Sterne was supported through Cambridge by a
respectable relative, and went into the Church because the Church
was where respectable Sternes went. As a churchman he became
noted not for his piety but for his odd frankness about piety, his
tendency to amend biblical texts, and his unchurchly companions,
such as the Demoniacs. The Demoniacs fiddled, piped, told Rabelai-

sian stories, and drank, and Sterne was a prominent Demoniac when he was not being churchly, or amorous. Cross reports that when Sterne married he was thought of in his neighborhood as a rake, and was criticized, not unreasonably, for marrying the woman, Elizabeth Lumley, instantly after her receipt of a small fortune. Sterne's letters to Elizabeth at the time were extravagantly romantic, with an arch awareness of their extravagance:

> We will be as merry and innocent as our first parents. . . . Let the human tempest and hurricane rage at a distance. . . . No planetary influence shall reach us, but that which presides and cherishes the sweetest flowers. God preserve us! How delightful this prospect in idea!

Such cleverness did not always conceal his bad temper, or his righteousness, which for some years extended to his relationship with his ill-bred mother. Upon the appearance of Elizabeth's fortune, not only did the marriage take place but Sterne's mother came right over from Ireland and settled expensively into his life (as did his sister). His mother provoked him to extended and humorless arguments, by letter, with his church superior, in which he tried to justify his intent to kick her out. The arguments were of a kind that, when conducted by others, he soon came to satirize for their base in self-interest, perhaps without realizing—at least at first—that he was partly satirizing himself. His most seminal pre-Shandean satire was an in-house political attack, *The History of a Good Watch-Coat.*

The tract was mainly an attack on a church entrepreneur who had recently lost two fairly fat preferments (one to Sterne himself) that he had intrigued at length to get. The intrigue had been fomented by all sides, but Sterne's central villain had stirred up more fuss than the others. Sterne presented him, in a heavy allegory, as a greedy little "parish clerk" who had wanted a certain spacious watch-coat, owned by his superior, for several homey purposes, then had taken the coat without permission, and had cut it up *for* those purposes (one purpose being a petticoat for his wife). Sterne attacked him for his haste and presumptuousness, then attacked the other intriguers, too, for making so much of so little. Nor was he done then, since in a "key" that he appended to the tract itself he proceeded to introduce several learned critics of the tract—false learning was always a favorite target for him—and have them somberly discuss the meaning of the coat-stealing allegory. Here he proposed that it was (1) really about an altercation between the king and queen of France, with the kings of England and Prussia also implicated; (2) really about various recent partition treaties in Europe (symbolized by the cutting up of the coat); and (3) *possibly* about an exceedingly minor and local parish matter.

The minor and local church officials involved were predictably less than pleased with the tract and the "key," and Cross reports that Sterne "heeded the advice of his clerical friends that the Romance be suppressed." But it had already been printed, so had also to be burned. It was, and though Sterne saved a few copies, its loss was painful to him. It immediately preceded the writing of *Tristram Shandy*, and, being his first real literary venture, can be thought of as the provocation for it. He was suddenly inclined to think of himself as a literary—a suppressed literary—man.

Then, too, he must suddenly have been aware, though here I speculate, of what was wrong with the tract: its heavy political tread, its insistent local targeting, and its ethical superficiality. He must have wanted to do something more spacious, so cast about among his acquaintances for a cast of characters to work with outside the frame of the church incident.

Most of all, he must have been developing at this time a rather urgent awareness of his own character, with its eccentricities, vices, what you will. Seventeen fifty-nine was a heavy year for him, not only in the Church, but also at home and in the private places where he was conducting an affair. Cross does not mention the affair until after reporting on wife Elizabeth's sudden madness, but other scholars have thought the madness was caused by the affair. In any event, Sterne found himself, right at the time of the tract-burning, with a wife who thought she was the queen of Bohemia. He rose to the occasion by "treating her as such, with all the respect due to a crowned head," but he was soon writing, writing, writing. Meanwhile he was "flirting"—the word is Cross's—with Miss Catherine Fourmantelle. It was a busy time, 1759.

Being out on a limb in the church and at home, Sterne *needed* to write. He sat in his study with Swift, Burton, and the others, and did so. He wrote, then walked outside as if to go to town, then thought of something new to put down, and rushed back in. One of his most quoted remarks in *Tristram Shandy* was that the best way to write was to write the first sentence and then the second, but this principle—which can be attributed to Locke, if need be—had behind it a directive intensity that belied simple randomness. A later moralist critic—Sidney Lee of the *Dictionary of National Biography*—said that writing *Tristram Shandy* "dissipated most of his cares." It may have done that, but it also drove him to examine those cares as he never had before. And the examination was not just recreational, for as he said in Book IV, he was studying "the triumph of slight incidents over the mind"—that is, the mind's "flight behind the scenes." Such study *was* study. It was directed, though wildly.

What was it directed at? It was directed at finding a key, but this time a real key, a key to character, real character. It was especially directed at the sources of character, just as the probings of psycho-biographers are now directed, and this psychological connection is important despite the great dissimilarities. In both cases the basic impulse can be seen to be investigative, though in Sterne's case the investigative was uncomfortably mixed with show-and-tell. By 1759 Sterne had developed a thorough fascination with the individual—his lonely, splendid, individual soul—and wanted to examine that odd entity.

He therefore distanced himself somewhat, at least for the moment, from public harangues and posturing, in favor of comic, but only semicomic, meditations upon the inner man. And early in *Tristram Shandy* he gave Walter Shandy two axioms about human individuals that must be taken as thoroughly Sterne's, and that lie behind his mode of character portrayal throughout the work. First, "Every man's wit must come from every man's own soul, and no other body's"; and second, "An ounce of a man's own wit [is] worth a ton of other people's."

The axioms have a defiance about them. In 1759 Sterne's own wit and soul were at last on their own—and he seemed pleased that they were—but they were on their own under the condition of being surrounded by complainers *about* their independence, from the mother and wife to the church persons Sterne had attacked. In some guise or another, the complainers all seem to appear in *Tristram Shandy*, but they are subordinate to Sterne himself, who appears as four of its characters—the most sympathetic ones: Walter Shandy, Uncle Toby, Parson Yorick, and the about-to-be Tristram, who is narrator. I mean simply that these four have a soul-center of sorts, and *Tristram Shandy* is a work in search, if falteringly, of that center.

On its first page Sterne proposes that a man's life is permanently conditioned by what the parents had on their minds at the moment of begetting. The proposal is partly a joke—and even Freud will not later locate such influence so specifically—but Sterne is aware of his joking being more than joking. He wants us to be amused by it, and amused a few pages later when he has the wife declare—the subject is still the moment of begetting—that the clock needs to be wound; but he does not want us to be so amused as to think there is nothing *in* the notion. The same can be said of Sterne's connecting the soul with "animal spirits," and making a similar connection later (in *A Sentimental Journey*) of the soul with "the little interests below." Sterne was searching out, between Shandean frivolities, the soul's *source* in animal spirits and little interests. And if I read him rightly, he thought he had found it. At the same time, he found that the spirits or interests had been distracted, at the moment of conception, by the wife's clock-winding remark, so that they were "scattered and dispersed" forever after.

And Tristram's soul was therefore also scattered and dispersed forever after; and so was Sterne's own soul, and the soul of his closest alias, Yorick. From that moment, none of them could ever quite settle on what or who he was, but each became a creature of many roles, many moods, many understandings, a creature with identity problems. This was not just Shandean foolery.

Nor was it just mild pornographic foolery when Sterne made the soul's origins sexual. The sexual emphasis in *Tristram Shandy* was hardly new, even in the eighteen century, and even from a vicar, but it was an odd component for the time in the portrayal of individual character development. A polite word that Sterne used for sex, sometimes more pointedly than others, covered up the sexual elements, but not much. The word was *sentiment* or *sentimental*.

He is commonly credited with having been the first user of the word in the sense in which we now apply it to sentimental eighteenth- and nineteenth-century novels, but that sense is distractingly prissy. Much closer to his sense is his description of his feelings for Miss Fourmantelle in 1759, in which he speaks of "that tender and delicious sentiment, which ever mixes in friendship, where there is a difference in sex." It is *that* kind of sentiment that was in his head when he took on *Tristram Shandy*.

Naturally, though, there was much else in his head at the same time, with the result that the opposing Sterne schools have not, to my knowledge, argued the point of the sentimentally sexual as much as they should have. I think that in both *Tristram Shandy* and *A Sentimental Journey* (which I am approaching) the sexual was, for Sterne, sentiment's center, and I see it being acknowledged as such, over and over in these works, acknowledged or seen to be lurking conspicuously behind a pillar like a villain in an old comedy. The arguments and horseplay in the comedy would go on, center stage, but the player behind the pillar was someone Sterne would keep his eye on at all times.

He wrote rapidly. In a few months he had the first two books of *Tristram* in hand, and they were the books that made his name. He was on a roll. Aside from the character of unborn Tristram himself, he had five really significant personages to deal with—the four who were largely himself, plus the stupid Dr. Slop—and each of these was an abrupt stimulus-response system. Their systems were partly humourous in the old sense, yet Sterne seldom mentioned the old humours, and he made each of the characters, beyond his or her particular humour, unpredictable and individual, with a psychic history. He tried to show us that these characters had earned their system-structures through strange, small incidents in the past that resonated through their lives.

And he did not make those incidents merely pat and arbitrary, like Don Quixote's having read too many chivalric romances. Right from the beginning, with the Sunday night clock-winding, Sterne was searching out particular odd events and feelings in the depths of his characters' private lives, and meditating, though sometimes like a zany, upon their meaning.

He was meditating investigatively. He was analyzing his whole cluster of selves, and finding, for instance, that the demands upon his vicar self were constantly up against the little interests below. For some time he had been dealing with the little interests in his own church life—that is, in his sermons. But now he was moving away from the genre of sermon to that of the novel, or autobiography— whatever *Tristram Shandy* was—and finding the shift a happy one. He found he could even include within the work old sermons he had actually given and have his characters comment on them.

It was such a sermon, presented as Yorick's but read by Corporal Trim, that contained the phrase, "the little interests below." Those little interests, Yorick pointed out, made trusting to one's conscience like a good Protestant difficult. But for one's conscience, those little interests might lead a soul into all the pits of darkness; and sometimes they led the soul there with the *aid* of one's conscience. The conscience could be distracted, deceived, misled by the little interests.

The conscience was not always reliable, because the little interests were really big interests. With papist Dr. Slop angrily in attendance as Corporal Trim read the sermon, Yorick steered a narrow course between papist reliance on the Church as conscience, and Protestant reliance on a fallible private conscience. He managed to demolish Dr. Slop, but he nearly demolished his own church as well. The sermon's conclusion pointed to the need for an extremely alert, wide-ranging conscience, but its vigor was in describing the little interests. The little interests made cheating the conscience easy. The little interests dreamed up moral reasons for whatever served them.

Even in Yorick's sermon, then, Sterne was probing an emergent order, an order denying surface order and subsisting beneath the surface, an order whose study now is given over mostly to psychiatrists, or to those who think they are. But of course Sterne did not pick up his interest in it from psychiatrists, except perhaps from Robert Burton. He picked it up from the comic authors he admired, including Shakespeare, authors who made capital of the triumph of low motives in man, or of the absurdity of high motives in man: Rabelais, Cervantes. One can think of the stage aside—of villains saying what heroines want to hear, then turning to the audience and muttering, "Ha! That will do it!" One can think of Sancho Panza blowing away, with earthy remarks, Don Quixote's fantasies. The tradition of the low was literarily long and sane in Sterne's consciousness. Pathology had not entered into it except perhaps in the guise of hypocritical moralists—perhaps some in Sterne's own church. Thus Tristram's primal soul-crushing at birth made him (and Yorick) not a mental case, but a pleasantly unpredictable savant. And Uncle Toby's impotence made him not a sad neurotic, but a human, slightly nutty enthusiast. And Walter Shandy's obsessions were civilized, even occasionally productive of wisdom. In other words, the effects of the little interests below were benign in Sterne's characters. The characters became not models, but humans, impure but healthily so. They appeared open and transparent before the reader, not hermetic as would be the case when Freud got hold of their kind.

Tristram Shandy was nowhere neat and symmetrical, or pure, because the interests below were in charge. Nothing could go forward properly—not even syntax—because mental impediments out of the depths kept appearing. The impediments were mostly pleasant, though, and the disorder was attractive, enforcing the reader's sense of openness and honesty in the characters, even the character of the stupid Dr. Slop. In *Sentimental Journey through France and Italy*, Sterne reached for the same tone, and tried to simplify the confusion by having just one main character, Yorick. But some of the openness and honesty was rendered suspect by an overlay of clear commercial intent in the work. Sterne was clearly writing a book to sell, and had discovered what would.

I should say in parenthesis that Sterne's critics disagree here, some saying that, yes, he had become callous, a merchant of the sentimental, and some saying that he had himself become pathologically sentimental. I suppose that the latter, who include Professor Cross, were quietly disapproving of his sexual drift, but at any rate the one hero, Yorick, was not to be distinguished from Sterne himself.* Yorick was quickly, arbitrarily, and oversimplistically distinguished, right at the start, from all other possible travelers—idle, inquisitive, lying, proud, vain, splenetic, and so on—by virtue of his being literally led through his travels by his sentiments. He had a diversionary—that is, nonsexual—attack of sentiment at the very beginning, when, though feeling generous, he impetuously *declined* a good monk's plea for alms; but soon he was in the hands of sex. While he was negotiating for the rental of a carriage, the carriage owner left him for a moment with an unknown lady and he found himself in the carriage with the lady, holding, for no apparent reason, her hand. Then he walked into a bookstore for a copy of Shakespeare, and emerged with *un jeune fille*. The *jeune fille* led him into many adventures (none of his own doing), which even involved the re-entrance of the lady in the carriage. So fate, it seemed, was intervening in his life at every corner, but was always helped to its interventions by "sentiment."

The results of the sexual dominance of sentiment was asserted and summed up at the volume's end. There fate decreed that Yorick share a room for a night with a proud female in a crowded inn. Fate also decreed that they share not just the room but two beds close together. The female then decreed—and a document was drawn up to clarify her wishes—that a curtain be put up between them, that he wear a pair of black breeches all night, and that he speak not a word until dawn. Inadvertently at 1:00 A.M.—though surely the little interests below had something to do with it—he muttered, "Oh my God!" and the

---

*Sterne's letters from France and Italy during his real trip to those countries point to the dominance of the commercial motive in *A Sentimental Journey*. The real trip, as described in the letters, is not even remotely like Yorick's trip.

lady informed him that he had "broken the treaty." They disputed the point, and *un fille de chambre*, fearing hostilities, entered. What next? The *fille de chambre* "got herself into the narrow passage which separated them, and advanced so far up as to be in a line betwixt her mistress and me—so that when I stretched out my hand"—he was merely gesturing to prove a point—"I caught hold of the fille de chambre's ——."

End of volume. An eighteenth-century Freudian slip? Whatever one calls it, it was a conspicuously hoked-up ending, reflecting the volume's farcical tone generally. Of *Tristram Shandy* Sterne had said, " 'Tis a picture of myself,'"* but of *A Sentimental Journey* he should have been obliged to add that he was writing of the self in him that was devoted to money and *les jeunes filles*.

◆ ◆

The Romantic Revolution turned out to be all about Mr. Shandy's one-wit, one-soul axioms, though their application by Mr. Shandy was to a more limited event, the near fatal squeezing of Tristram's soul (located by Mr. Shandy in the cerebellum) by the mother's pelvis and Dr. Slop's forceps. The Romantic Revolution had a number of causes in tow, and Mr. Shandy might have disliked them, but one of the causes was the self's independence. That independence meant a great deal to religion (think of Jonathan Edwards, who was said to have been "awakened" by it when he found it asserted in John Locke), to social thinking (remember the Benthamites), to literature (the mirror becoming the lamp), and to the Shandeans, an odd bunch whose thoughts about it are not even classifiable. *Tristram Shandy* is, like its author's self, a notably independent work, and its greatness lies partly in its page-by-page demonstration of independence. Imagine putting the preface in Book III, chapter 20.

One hundred and thirty years later, Sidney Lee in the *Dictionary of National Biography* was unhappy about Sterne's independence, like Johnson, Goldsmith, and the others earlier. Lee's account of Sterne's life is thorough and detailed, and at the end of it he becomes gracious enough to acknowledge Sterne's genius, briefly. But throughout he is steadily critical of the improprieties that started Sterne on his literary way. As a Victorian, Lee was morally troubled by them, and as a

*From Lewis Perry Curtis's introduction to *The Letters of Laurence Sterne* (Oxford, 1935).

creator of dictionary biographies, he found it inconvenient for genius to be so wayward. He was annoyed with the disorder in Sterne's approach to real, as well as literary, lives, and managed to miss the causes of disorder that Sterne was searching for. He did not *look* for causes, but simply blamed the impropriety on Sterne's permanently unstable temperament, noting that even as a child Sterne was moved "to uncontrollable tears and laughter" as he read the *Iliad*. He traced the instability right up to Sterne's career as a parson, there finding him guilty of "light-hearted indifference . . . [to his] sacred functions" and inattentive to his marital obligations. He did not probe the inattentiveness, the indifference. He merely disapproved. There was, he clearly felt, decorum to be observed, and a proper conscience would have recognized the need for observance.

For our un-Victorian time, Sterne's conscience remains a matter of concern, but the concern has changed. One still does not know quite how to have him, but one does not worry about approving him so much as understanding him, understanding his intentions. One must worry particularly—without finding a final answer—about how seriously Sterne thought of his volumes as forms of self-analysis. I have not found a good psychobiographer who has dedicated him- or herself to that problem, though there may be one. My own understanding of Sterne stops far short of an answer, with simply a vision of a man wiser—for reasons having, or not having, to do with forceps— than his critics, wise beyond the clutches of custom. I think of him, in the moments of writing *Tristram Shandy*, as living with the delusive novelty of independence like a young explorer on a brand new planet. Writing itself had become exploration for him then; his circumstances had somehow driven him to the wonders of it. So he did his exploring in an armchair, finding that he could do what he wanted there, in a world where, otherwise, he was having limited luck doing what he wanted. The finding bowled him over. (He must have been someone who laughed at his own jokes.) He found that with no trouble at all he could write, as if autobiographically, about prenatal affairs, and have the narrator tell the story as if he were consciously, a graduate of Cambridge, there. He found that he could write a story that was not a story at all but a long interruption of one. He found that Mr. Shandy could solve all of mankind's ideological problems without even going to London (his legal agreement with his wife, about *not* going to London for Tristram's birth, took four pages), and that Uncle Toby could fight all the battles of Europe at home. In other words he found the life of the self to be suddenly spacious to a degree he had not previously imagined. The self did not even have to make its printed statements orderly, judicious, well balanced. There is nothing in English, before the stream-of-consciousness era, more jumpy and less predictable than Sterne's prose at its best, and nothing more convincing.

I do not find in Sterne's own words any explanations of his psychic roots other than those he supplies for Tristram; hence I find no explanation of the causes of his wonders. But it is clear to me that he was in fact the phenomenon that the reading public took him for, all of a heap, in 1760. His wonders made him probably the major eighteenth-century English figure to be directing his attention to characters *not* concerned with, in Johnson's phrase, "the downfall of kingdoms and the revolutions of empires," but with the individual in the privacies of "sentiment."

There was the domesticity of Pepys as well, the commoner-concerns of Defoe, and the plain dailiness of other writers of the time, but the strange probings of Shandy Hall stand out above them all. The English were preparing to be eccentrically sedentary, despite their colonizing leaders, but none of the English eccentrics were more comfortably separated from "affairs" than Sterne's characters. With them, the local and familial not only took precedence over state matters but suffered a sea-change and became matters that went beneath the local and familial.

And biography? It was such a loose genre anyway, and so surrounded by literary figures like Moll Flanders and Colonel Jack—or at higher levels Belinda, Lady Wishfort, and the not-very-high Squire Western—that it could not have kept its doors shut on what Johnson called "the minute details of private life" even if there had been a Commissioner of Biography.

But biography was not destined to follow along with Sterne's kind of privacies for a long time, and when it did, it did not do so clearly. There is no solid connection between Sterne's probings and those of the psychobiographers, and to make the connection solid is to misrepresent it. Yet to deny the connection is a mistake too. Sterne hit a vein that had not been well explored before him, and the popularity he enjoyed showed, if nothing else, that it was worth exploring. What is surprising is that the vein was so generally taken as merely comic. It was misunderstood, and perhaps still is; hence it was not seen as a serious approach to character.

One feature of the misunderstanding is understandable, though, and I may have encouraged it by emphasizing Sterne's eccentricity. He was eccentric all right, and he was the author of Walter Shandy's one-wit, one-soul axioms, but his self problems were not particularly narcissistic. He was not, I would say, in love with himself, either as a professionally humble Christian or as an entrepreneur, Demoniac, and chaser of women. He was not in love with his sentiments; he just had them, recognized them, probed them, and capitalized on them, when he was not being run by them. So he was able to look at them with a measure of detachment. He was able to contemplate personality, even his own, impersonally, a prime requirement for any biographer, who must stand far enough away from his subject to see him. Not that Sterne *was* a biographer. He was just a deviant, impure model of one, a mock-up of what a biographer would be if he did not take on great public figures, and if he looked not at his subjects' performances but at their sentiments. As such, though, he pointed the way inadvertently to a *group* approach to sentiments. The little interests below composed the sentiments and were, though deeply private and singular, also deeply shared.

One word for the sentiments now is *archetypal*, but Sterne, if he had thought of himself as a groupy, might have preferred to call them Christian. And in a Shandean way they were. Despite Johnson, Sidney Lee, and the rest, Sterne was indeed a moralist of sorts, and no committed and intelligent moralist can ever be a full-fledged narcissist, *or* pornographer, *or* private entrepreneur.

Appendix: Johnson on Biography

Whose works the beautiful and base contain;
Of vice and virtue more instructive rules,
Than all the sober sages of the schools.

FRANCIS.

All joy or sorrow for the happiness or calamities of others is produced by an act of the imagination, that realizes the event however fictitious, or approximates it however remote, by placing us, for a time, in the condition of him whose fortune we contemplate; so that we feel, while the deception lasts, whatever motions would be excited by the same good or evil happening to ourselves.

Our passions are therefore more strongly moved, in proportion as we can more readily adopt the pains or pleasure proposed to our minds, by recognizing them as once our own, or considering them as naturally incident to our state of life. It is not easy for the most artful writer to give us an interest in happiness or misery, which we think ourselves never likely to feel, and with which we have never yet been made acquainted. Histories of the downfall of kingdoms, and revolutions of empires, are read with great tranquility; the imperial tragedy pleases common auditors only by its pomp of ornament, and grandeur of ideas; and the man whose faculties have been engrossed by business, and whose heart never flut-

Reprinted from *Rambler*, no. 60 (October 13, 1750).

tered but at the rise and fall of stocks, wonders how the attention can be seized, or the affection agitated by a tale of love.

Those parallel circumstances, and kindred images, to which we readily conform our minds, are, above all other writings, to be found in narratives of the lives of particular persons; and therefore no species of writing seems more worthy of cultivation than biography, since none can be more delightful or more useful, none can more certainly enchain the heart by irresistible interest, or more widely diffuse instruction to every diversity of condition.

The general and rapid narratives of history, which involve a thousand fortunes in the business of a day, and complicate innumerable instances in one great transaction, afford few lessons applicable to private life, which derives its comforts and its wretchedness from the right or wrong management of things which nothing but their frequency makes considerable, *Parva, si non fiunt quotidiae*, says Pliny, and which can have no place in those relations which never descend below the consultations of senates, the motions of armies, and the schemes of conspirators.

I have often thought that there has rarely passed a life of which a judicious and faithful narrative would not be useful. For, not only every man has, in the mighty mass of the world, great numbers in the same condition with himself, to whom his mistakes and miscarriages, escapes and expedients, would be of immediate and apparent use; but there is such an uniformity in the state of man, considered apart from adventitious and separable decorations and disguises, that there is scarce any possibility of good or ill, but is common to human kind. A great part of the time of those who are placed at the greatest distance by fortune, or by temper, must unavoidably pass in the same manner; and though, when the claims of nature are satisfied, caprice, and vanity, and accident, begin to produce discriminations and peculiarities, yet the eye is not very heedful, or quick, which cannot discover the same causes still terminating their influences in the same effects, though sometimes accelerated, sometimes retarded, or perplexed by multiplied combinations. We are all prompted by the same motives, all deceived by the same fallacies, all animated by hope, obstructed by danger, entangled by desire, and seduced by pleasure.

It is frequently objected to relations of particular lives, that they are not distinguished by any striking or wonderful vicissitudes. The scholar who passed his life among books, the merchant who conducted only his own affairs, the priest, whose sphere of action was not extended beyond that of his duty, are considered as no proper objects of publick regard, however they might have excelled in their several stations, whatever might have been their learning, integrity and piety. But this notion arises from false measures of excellence and dignity, and must be eradicated by considering, that, in the esteem of uncorrupted reason, what is of most use is of most value.

It is, indeed, not improper to take honest advantages of prejudice, and to gain attention by a celebrated name; but the business of a biographer is often to pass slightly over those performances and incidents, which produce vulgar greatness, to lead the thoughts into domestick privacies, and display the minute details of daily life, where exterior appendages are cast aside, and men excel each other only by prudence and by virtue. The account of Thuanus is, with great propriety, said by its author to have been written that it might lay open to posterity the private and familiar character of that man, *cujus ingenium et candorem ex ipsius scriptis sunt olim semper miraturi*, whose candour and genius will to the end of time be by his writings preserved in admiration.

There are many invisible circumstances which, whether we read as inquirers after natural or moral knowledge, whether we intend to enlarge our science, or increase our virtue, are more important than publick occurrences. Thus Salust, a great master of nature, has not forgot, in his account of Catiline, to remark that *his walk was now quick, and then again slow*, as an indication of a mind revolving something with violent commotion. Thus the story of Melancthon affords a striking lecture on the value of time, by informing us, that when he made an appointment, he expected not only the hour, but the minute to be fixed, that the day might not run out in the idleness of suspense; and all the plans and enterprizes of De Wit are now of less importance to the world, than that part of his personal character which represents him as *careful of his health*, and *negligent of his life*.

But biography has often been allotted to writers who seem very little acquainted with the nature of their task, or very negligent about the performance. They rarely afford any other account than might be collected from publick papers, but imagine themselves writing a life when they exhibit a chronological series of actions or preferments; and so little regard the manners or behaviour of their heroes, that more knowledge may be gained of a man's real character, by a short conversation with one of his servants, than from a formal and studied narrative, begun with his pedigree, and ended with his funeral.

If now and then they condescend to inform the world of particular facts, they are not always so happy as to select the most important. I know not well what advantage posterity can receive from the only circumstance by which Tickell has distinguished Addison from the rest of mankind, *the irregularity of his pulse*; nor can I think myself overpaid for the time spent in reading the life of Malherb, by being able to relate, after the learned biographer [H. de Racan], that Malherb had two predominant opinions; one, that the looseness of a single woman might destroy all her boast of ancient descent; the other, that the French beggars made use very improperly and barbarously of the phrase *noble Gentleman*, because either word included the sense of both.

There are, indeed, some natural reasons why these narratives are often written by such as were not likely to give much instruction or delight, and why most accounts of particular persons are barren and useless. If a life be delayed till interest and envy are at an end, we may hope for impartiality, but must expect little intelligence; for the incidents which give excellence to biography are of a volatile and evanescent kind, such as soon escape the memory, and are rarely transmitted by tradition. We know how few can portray a living acquaintance, except by his most prominent and observable particularities, and the grosser features of his mind; and it may be easily imagined how much of this little knowledge may be lost in imparting it, and how soon a succession of copies will lose all resemblance of the original.

If the biographer writes from personal knowledge, and makes haste to gratify the publick curiosity, there is danger lest his interest, his fear, his gratitude, or his tenderness, overpower his fidelity, and tempt him to conceal, if not to invent. There are many who think it an act of piety to hide the faults or failings of their friends, even when they can no longer suffer by their detection; we therefore see whole ranks of characters adorned with uniform panegyrick, and not to be known from one another, but by extrinsick and casual circumstances. "Let me remember," says Hale, "when I find myself inclined to pity a criminal, that there is likewise a pity due to the country." If we owe regard to the memory of the dead, there is yet more respect to be paid to knowledge, to virtue, and to truth.

Primary Readings

The main texts I have had reference to, and quote from, are described under each heading below. Only when the source is a peripheral text, and not clearly acknowledged, have I supplied a specific footnote in the text.

Introduction

Aristotle. *Aristotle's Poetics*. Translated by S. H. Butcher. London: Macmillan, 1898.

Aubrey, John. *Aubrey's Brief Lives*. Edited by Oliver Lawson Dick, with an introduction by Edmund Wilson. Ann Arbor: University of Michigan Press, 1957.

Burckhardt, Jacob. *The Civilization of the Renaissance in Italy*. 1860. Reprint. New York: Harper, 1958.

Gosse, Edmund. "Biography." *Encyclopaedia Britannica*, 11th ed. (1910).

———. *Father and Son: A Study of Two Temperaments*. 1907. Reprint. New York: Norton, 1963.

Mierow, Charles. *The Hallowed Flame*. Evanston: Principia Press of Illinois, 1956.

Pinto, Vivian De Sola. *English Biography in the Seventeenth Century*. London: G. G. Harrop, 1951.

Strachey, Lytton. *Eminent Victorians*. New York: Modern Library, 1933.

Plutarch

All quotations from Plutarch's *Lives of the Noble Grecians and Romans* are from the Dryden translation, as presented in the Modern Library edition

(New York, 1935). Quotations from other works by Plutarch are from Harvard University Press's Loeb Library volumes of Plutarch.

Aelfric

Aelfric's *Lives of the Saints*, edited by Walter W. Skeat (London: N. Trübner & Co., 1881–1900), has been my main source, supplemented by *The Homilies of Aelfric: A Supplementary Collection*, edited by John C. Pope (London and New York: Oxford University Press, 1967–68), and by a strange Aelfric text, *Exameron Anglice; or, The Old English Hexameron*, edited by Samuel John Crawford (Hamburg: H. Grand, 1921). Background volumes are as follows:

Adamnan. *Life of Saint Columba*. Edited by William Reeves. Edinburgh, 1874.

Asser, John. *Asser's Life of King Alfred*. Translated by Simon Keynes and Michael Lapidge. New York: Penguin, 1983.

Aurelius, Marcus. *Meditations*. New York: Heritage Press, 1956.

Gregg, Robert, trans. *Athanasius: The Life of Antony and the Letter to Marcellinus*. Ramsey, N.J.: Paulist Press, 1980.

Hannah, Ian C. *Christian Monasticism*. London: Allen and Unwin, 1924.

Hunt, James. *Aelfric*. New York: Twayne, 1972.

Jacobus de Varagine. *Legenda Aurea* [The Golden Legend]. 1474. In *Lives of the Saints*, as Englished by William Caxton. New York: AMS Press, 1973.

John of Salerno. *St. Odo of Cluny*. Translated by Dom Gerard Sitwell. London: Sheed and Ward, 1958.

Misch, Georg. *A History of Autobiography in Antiquity*. 1907. Reprint. London: Routledge and Paul, 1951.

Morris, John N. *Versions of the Self*. New York: Basic Books, 1966.

Nicolson, Harold. *The Development of English Biography*. London: Hogarth Press, 1927.

White, Caroline. *Aelfric*. 1898. Reprint. Garden City, N.Y.: Doubleday, Anchor, 1974.

Machiavelli, Cellini, Vasari

I have referred to the Modern Library edition of Machiavelli's *The Prince and The Discourses* (New York, 1940), which contains an introduction by Max Lerner; the Penguin paperback edition of Cellini's *Autobiography*, translated by George Bull (New York, 1956); and the Penguin paperback edition of Vasari's *Lives of the Artists*, also translated by Bull (New York,

1965), who provides an excellent introduction to both of the last two works. I have also referred to the complete edition of Vasari's *Lives*, published by Abrams (New York, 1977). Other sources:

Freud, Sigmund. *Leonardo da Vinci and a Memory of His Childhood*. Translated by Alan Tyson. New York: Norton, 1964.

Machiavelli, Nicolò. *Mandragola*. Translated by A. and H. Paolucci. Indianapolis: Bobbs-Merrill, 1957.

Pulver, Jeffrey. *Machiavelli*. London: H. Joseph Ltd., 1937.

Seymour, Charles, Jr. *Michelangelo's David: A Search for Identity*. Pittsburgh: University of Pittsburgh Press, 1967.

Uccello, Paolo. *The Complete Work of Paolo Uccello*. With an introduction by John Pope-Hennessy, who quotes Ruskin on Uccello. New York: Phaidon, 1969.

Chronicles, Holinshed, Shakespeare

The *Anglo-Saxon Chronicle* is now available in a useful and brief comparative-text format (it has been passed down to us in many shapes and sizes) edited by Dorothy Whitlock (London: Eyre and Spottswood, 1961). Other sources:

Bede. *History of the English Church and People*. Edited and translated by Leo Sherley-Price. New York: Penguin, 1955.

Booth, Stephen. *The Book Called Holinshed's Chronicles*. San Francisco: Book Club of California, 1968.

Froissart, Jean. *The Chronicle of Froissart*. Translated by John Bourchier. 6 vols. 1901–3. Reprint. New York: AMS Press, 1967.

Holinshed, Raphael. *Chronicles of England, Scotland, and Ireland*. 1577–78. Reprint of Henry Ellis's edition, 1807–8. 6 vols. New York: AMS Press, 1976.

Mears, William. *The Castrations of the Last Edition of Holinshed's Chronicle*. London, 1723.

Nietzsche, Friedrich. *The Philosophy of Nietzsche* [including *Beyond Good and Evil*]. New York: Modern Library, 1954.

Stoll, E. E. *Art and Artifice in Shakespeare*. Cambridge: Cambridge University Press, 1933.

Samuel Johnson

There are many reprints of the individual works of Johnson, but his complete works were available to me only in a nineteenth-century edition, in microscopic print, edited, with an essay on his life and genius, by

Arthur Murphy (*The Works of Samuel Johnson, LL.D.*, American ed., 2 vols. [New York: Harper, 1859]). Murphy's interesting prefatory biography has been my source for comments on Johnson's conviction that biography was aimed to "advance" readers in virtue, and on Johnson's causing his friends to "tremble" when he undertook his biography of Milton. Another good source has been *Johnson on Johnson*, edited by John Wain (New York: Dutton, 1976).

As for Boswell, the Oxford edition of his *Life of Johnson* (1953) has been used, as has the Viking *Portable Johnson and Boswell* (New York, 1947), edited by Louis Kronenberger, which contains Boswell's account of his meetings with Rousseau. Other sources:

Bate, W. Jackson. *Samuel Johnson*. New York: Harcourt, 1977.
Krutch, Joseph Wood. *Samuel Johnson*. New York: Holt, 1944.
Macaulay, Thomas B. "Johnson." In Macaulay's *Prose and Poetry*, edited by G. M. Young. Cambridge: Harvard University Press, 1967.
Savage, Richard. *The Poetical Works*. Edited by Clarence Tracy. Cambridge: Cambridge University Press, 1962.
Wain, John. *Samuel Johnson: A Biography*. New York: Viking, 1975.

James Boswell

Other than the *Portable Johnson and Boswell* and Boswell's *Life of Johnson* (editions cited above), I have had reference to the following:

Abbott, Claude Colleer. *Boswell*. Newcastle upon Tyne: Literary and Philosophical Society of Newcastle upon Tyne, 1946.
Boswell, James. *The Hypochondriack*. Edited by Margery Bailey. 2 vols. Stanford: Stanford University Press, 1928.
Ober, William. *Boswell's Clap, and Other Essays*. Carbondale: Southern Illinois University Press, 1979.

Laurence Sterne

Both *Tristram Shandy* and *A Sentimental Journey through France and Italy* are available in Penguin editions with excellent introductions (*Tristram*'s by Christopher Ricks [1967], *A Sentimental Journey*'s by A. Alvarez [1968]). Except where specifically indicated, I am indebted for biographical material, and for direct quotations about Sterne, to Wilbur L. Cross's biography, *The Life and Times of Laurence Sterne* (New Haven: Yale University Press, 1925). For quotations from Sterne's letters, I have drawn from *The Letters of Laurence Sterne*, edited by Lewis Perry Curtis (Oxford: Clarendon Press, 1935).

Index

REED WHITTEMORE is emeritus professor of English at the University of Maryland. He is the author of twelve books of poems and essays as well as a biography of William Carlos Williams. He has served twice as Consultant in Poetry at the Library of Congress.

Designed by Martha Farlow.

Composed by Professional Book Compositors, Inc., in Goudy Old Style, with display lines in Goudy Handtooled.

Printed by R. R. Donnelley & Sons Company on S. D. Warren's 50-lb. Cream White Sebago and bound in Joanna Kennett with Multicolor Antique endsheets.

Did biography exist as a genre before Dryden coined its name? Can Machiavelli, Shakespeare, or Laurence Sterne be numbered among its early practitioners? In delightful and surprising ways, Reed Whittemore traces the origins of biography in the lives and works of ancient, medieval, Renaissance, and early modern writers.

Taking their cue from Aristotle's *Poetics*, the early biographers chose as their subjects model human beings, individuals superior by reason of character and position. Unlike comedy, biography was grave in intent; yet unlike tragedy, it did not have to be purgative. Early biography aimed toward the purification of its audience by example, by the presentation of pure—or at least purified—lives. "All grave spirits have been purifiers of sorts," writes Whittemore. "In modern times Marx, Freud, . . . vegetarians, environmentalists, feminists, and minimalists might be mentioned as purifiers—not a cohesive group. All they have in common is an urge to improve us, together with a faith that improvement is possible."

The biographers Whittemore discusses also may seem an incohesive group, but they share a common line of descent. Plutarch's ethical biographies of Greek and Roman nobles established a tradition in which the form of a written life was determined by something beyond chronology—and in which the private self was subordinated to public acts and achievements. In this tradition Whittemore places Aelfric's *Lives of the Saints*, Vasari's *Lives of the Artists*, Holinshed's *Chronicles* of the rulers of England, Scotland, and Ireland, and Samuel Johnson's *Lives of the Poets*. But of special interest are writers whose status as biographers is less evident: